Daughters of the Empire

A Memoir of Life and Times in the British Raj

Iris Macfarlane

For Kate

Because she is interested in the family and I love her

CONTENTS

ILLUSTRATIONS

All photographs courtesy of the author.

Acknowledgements (from original edition)

I would like to thank the following who have read drafts of the book and made helpful comments - Andrew Morgan, Sally Dugan, Yona Friedman and John Davy. Also many thanks to Esha Béteille, Alan Macfarlane and especially to Sarah Harrison for help in various ways.

Forward by Alan Macfarlane

Like my mother Iris, I seek to understand myself in time. So I have naturally been fascinated by her account of four generations of women who lived between India and Britain from the middle of the nineteenth century to the later twentieth century. Yet I believe that this book is more than a purely family history, more than just a personal history of Iris, her mother Violet, her grand-mother Annie and great-grand-mother Maria. As Rumina Seth wrote in a review of the book, it is 'A class apart from the analyses of colonial novel and Raj films, Iris Macfarlane's narrative is a virtual social history of English life in India.'[2]

The days of the British Empire are now over, and the Jewel has been released from the Crown. It is becoming increasingly difficult to penetrate beneath the surface of those years, to see the emotions and ideas which shaped and were shaped by the imperial mission. I believe that my mother has had a number of advantages which has made it possible for her to do something very unusual.

Firstly there are her own talents. Sharp observation, a philosophical mind, cutting wit, self-depreciatory style, all these combined with beautiful writing have helped her to capture herself and her subjects. She can write with depth from her own experience, but also live past generations through that shared knowledge of the world of India and Britain. Then there is the unusual advantage of having a mother, Violet (who brought me up) a great story-teller and keeper of memories. In her late eighties, she handed down to Iris much of the information in this book and providing a bridge back to the later nineteenth century. Finally, my family is a great keeper of documents and photographs; sets of diaries, letters and other papers and illustrations give a first-hand richness to the hunt for these vanished worlds.

It is difficult to know what to compare this book to; a mixture of Trollope, Jane Austen and many of the classic accounts of the Raj I suppose. I believe that with its honesty, self-questioning and stringent critique it will be an invaluable source for those who are trying to understand the Raj. It also opens up the world of Victorian and Edwardian women, and more generally that world which gave birth to our own, whether we are British, Indian or world citizens in the aftermath of imperial expansion.

---

[2] *The Tribune*, New Delhi, 12 February 2006
[3] Reader in Historical Anthropology at the University of Cambridge
[4] Key works on these issues include: Strobel, M. and N. Chaudhuri (eds.) 1992 *Western Women and Imperialism. Complicity and resistance.* Bloomington: Indiana University Press; McClintock, A. 1995 *Imperial leather: race, gender, and sexuality in the colonial context.* London: Routledge; Cooper, F. and A. Stoler (eds.) 1997 *Tensions Of Empire.* Berkeley: University California Press; Clancy-Smith, J. & F. Gouda (eds.) 1998 *Domesticating The Empire: Race, Gender, & Family Life In French & Dutch Colonialism.* Charlottesville:

So when the book went out of print with Oxford University Press, who first published it in 2006 and the rights reverted to me as her son and literary executor, I decided to re-publish the work. I have retained the original text and photographs.

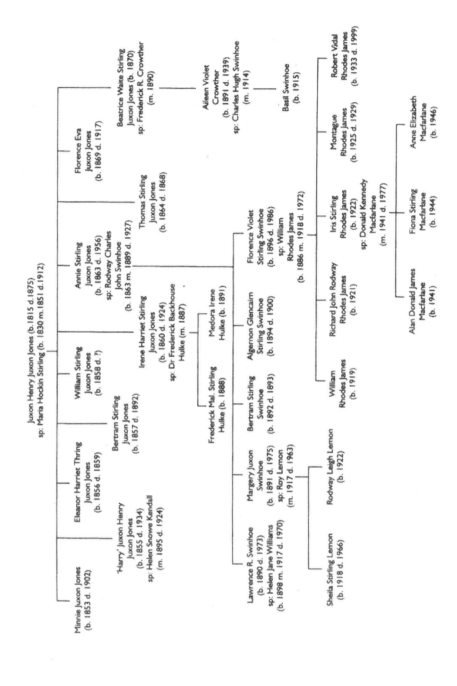

Juxon Henry Juxon Jones (b.1815 d.1875)
sp: Maria Hockin Stirling (b. 1830 m.1851 d.1912)

Minnie Juxon Jones
(b. 1853 d. 1902)

'Harry' Juxon Henry
Juxon Jones
(b. 1855 d. 1934)
sp: Helen Snowe Kendall
(m. 1895 d. 1924)

Eleanor Harriet Thring
Juxon Jones
(b. 1856 d. 1859)

Bertram Stirling
Juxon Jones
(b. 1857 d. 1892)

William Stirling
Juxon Jones
(b. 1858 d. ?)

Annie Stirling
Juxon Jones
(b. 1863 d. 1956)
sp: Rodway Charles
John Swinhoe
(b. 1863 m. 1889 d. 1927)

Florence Eva
Juxon Jones
(b. 1869 d. 1917)

Thomas Stirling
Juxon Jones
(b. 1864 d. 1868)

Beatrice Watre Stirling
Juxon Jones (b. 1870)
sp: Frederick R. Crowther
(m. 1890)

Aileen Violet
Crowther
(b. 1891 d. 1939)
sp: Charles Hugh Swinhoe
(m. 1914)

Basil Swinhoe
(b. 1915)

Irene Harriet Stirling
Juxon Jones
(b. 1860 d. 1924)
sp: Dr Frederick Backhouse
Hulke (m. 1887)

Frederick Mal. Stirling
Hulke (b. 1888)

Medora Irene
Hulke (b. 1891)

Lawrence R. Swinhoe
(b. 1890 d. 1973)
sp: Helen Jane Williams
(b. 1898 m. 1917 d. 1970)

Margery Juxon
Swinhoe
(b. 1891 d. 1975)
sp: Roy Lemon
(m. 1917 d. 1963)

Bertram Stirling
Swinhoe
(b. 1892 d. 1893)

Algernon Glencairn
Stirling Swinhoe
(b. 1894 d. 1900)

Florence Violet
Stirling Swinhoe
(b. 1896 d. 1986)
sp: William
Rhodes James
(b. 1886 m. 1918 d. 1972)

Sheila Stirling Lemon
(b. 1918 d. 1966)

Rodway Leigh Lemon
(b. 1922)

William
Rhodes James
(b. 1919)

Richard John Rodway
Rhodes James
(b. 1921)

Iris Stirling
Rhodes James
(b. 1922)
sp: Donald Kennedy
Macfarlane
(m. 1941 d. 1977)

Montague
Rhodes James
(b. 1925 d. 1929)

Robert Vidal
Rhodes James
(b. 1933 d. 1999)

Alan Donald James
Macfarlane
(b. 1941)

Fiona Stirling
Macfarlane
(b. 1944)

Anne Elizabeth
Macfarlane
(b. 1946)

9

Preface by Iris Macfarlane

I spent the last six years of her life with my mother, and every evening she would put her still neat ankles onto a footstool, sip whisky from a special bulb shaped glass, and talk about her family. Now that I am old myself I can understand the need to go over and over the incidents of a long life, and I recognise the glazed expressions on the faces of unwilling listeners, who give me the same lies I gave her when she asked if she had told me this before: "No, no, you haven't, tell me." She was ninety when she died, and so a little vaguer than I am. She was also a wonderful raconteur, who knew that she could reinvest the old dramas with life, however familiar the script.

Her story started in Mandalay in 1900 when she was four, and the bungalow echoed to the screams of her mother on opening a telegram. It told of the death in London of her brother Glen, six years old and left since babyhood with a working class family called Roberts in Blackheath. Later my mother heard more details of this disaster from her elder sister Margery. Glen had diphtheria and Margery was sent out into the streets to look for a doctor (did she knock on doors, ask passing strangers?) but when he arrived he could do little.

In spite of this tragedy my mother Violet was taken home and placed in the care of the same people. It was cold and dingy and boring she said, though they weren't unkind. Sometimes as a treat they went to tea with her grandmother Maria Juxon Jones, who with her two unmarried daughters Minnie and Flo lived at Palace Mansions a bus ride away. She loved the horse-drawn buses, and Grandmama allowed her to play with Glen's rocking horse which was kept as a sacred icon. The only contribution Palace Mansions had made to his life and death was in the shape of a tombstone. Tombstones were Maria's speciality.

My mother didn't know why she and her brother and sister weren't cared for at Palace Mansions, where there were servants as well as three unemployed women. Perhaps Glen wouldn't have died in its large clean rooms she surmised. He was one of three little boys sacrificed to the East, the other two little Tom who also died of diphtheria but in India, and little Monty, her own three year old who succumbed to dysentery. They left strands of hair and first teeth wrapped in tissue paper, and in Monty's case a large photograph, to be sadly handled until eventually the family forgot who they were.

After Blackheath there was a gap in the story, picking up when she was eighteen and at the Academy Schools at Burlington House. She had been parcelled out on various aunts and had only the sketchiest of schooling, the money having run out after her brother and sister were paid for. She started her art course in 1914 and loved it she said, becoming engaged to the star pupil and being quite excited about the war. Then her parents "dragged me out to Burma", she always used the word dragged, accompanied by a sweeping gesture, fists closed as around a braid of hair. Just before she left she met a man called Arnold, whose letters she kept in the cupboard by her chair.

Rereading them in old age she declared him to be the real love of her life. "I should have gone home and married him" she repeated over and over again, in spite of my snappy reminder that he died of pneumonia just after the armistice. She had kept her fiancé Harold's letters as well, carting all these around India on her many moves, until they ended up in the drawer of the mahogany cupboard she called the Georgian Gentleman. Harold's memory didn't enthuse her, perhaps because he stayed alive and visited her in his staid middle age. Through the British Legion she sent flowers to put on Arnold's grave in France until she died. She always grew pink and dewy eyed at his name, as if the seventy years that had passed since his death had melted away, and she was a girl again.

She often told of the night, Christmas Eve 1918 when she had woken to see his figure at the end of her bed in Upper Burma. He was wearing his uniform (khaki, she was vague about details) and soon after she got a letter to say that was the day he died. She was five months pregnant with her first child, but the shock didn't affect her fortunately. Strangely this momentous ghostly visit wasn't mentioned in her diary. Telling of it she would smile mysteriously, proudly, as being the possessor of psychic powers, and the recipient of a love that conquered space and death.

She had a photograph of herself in Burma soon before she left in 1922, and often described the occasion, the visit of HRH the Prince of Wales. Three months pregnant with me, she sat under an umbrella, waited on by white clad servants. The Prince was always late for the parties, polo matches, dance displays that were laid on for him, but they adored him nevertheless. My imminent arrival was the reason they left Burma, for a better-paid job in India. "How I loved Burma," my mother sighed, as of one dragged away again from a perfect world. I felt I had done the dragging.

In fact she loved India too, and produced many comic anecdotes about dinner parties, the servants one never knew what they would do next. She bred bullterriers and took leading roles in amateur dramatics, and of course with her psychic powers there were many stories of haunted houses and horses rearing where crimes had been committed. One particularly gruesome tale was of a tiger mauling, where the victim was plunged into a bath of iodine, but to no avail. Indians never featured in her life history except as cooks or Maharajahs, these last giving tennis parties where champagne flowed from silver buckets between sets.

When the six years we spent together ended with her death in 1986, I sat beside her for the last two weeks. She had a cancer operation and was in an Abbeyfield Home, and after a few months of typically courageous effort closed

11

her eyes and decided to give up. I sat holding her hand, my thumb on her pulse so as to know when dying had started. She wore the emerald engagement ring which was to go to her second daughter in law. The solitaire diamond was destined for her eldest son's wife the sapphire for her youngest's. Every evening she had taken out her jewel case to ponder who should get what. What if her grandson, who had a job in Germany, married one of Them? She wouldn't rest peacefully in her grave at the thought of her diamond on the finger of a foreigner.

As I sat beside her, her pulse beating softly and steadily under my thumb, my mind was full of the family she had talked of. They appeared to me in jerky flashes, like an old film, dressed in funny clothes and always having "barneys". They were an extremely quarrelsome lot the Joneses. There were scenes at meals when cutlery flew about and there were horrendous scenes when the contents of wills were disclosed. I remembered photographs she had shown me of scowling ladies, large busts heaving in front of the camera after what my mother appropriately called a Terrible Bust Up. I wondered why they were so permanently outraged, and thought of my grandmother telling me as a child of a Flaw in the family. I thought she meant floor, an unstable and dangerous room they walked across, Minnie and Flo and Beautiful Beatrice. She herself had somehow avoided this doomed apartment, being cheerful and charming. My mother's erratic temper (shouts and banged doors and unexpected slaps were the background to time spent with her) makes it seem that the flaw was in the family genes.

I suspected it also to be a symptom of the frustration felt by clever, spirited, beautiful women, cooped up with nothing to do. I wished I had asked my mother more about her aunts, and her own growing up. Now she slept peacefully, half waking at intervals to murmur of this and that. Her last words were accompanied by a slight lifting of the corners of her mouth as she whispered "The wheel went round and round" She even managed a faint circular movement of a wrist. I knew she was thinking of her honeymoon in Pagan, she and her bridegroom visiting pagodas in a bullock cart, and her looking down and seeing one of the wheels doing its last turn before falling off. She and Will were precipitated into the sand. "How we laughed and laughed" the story ended.

This ability to find the funny side of every situation however uncomfortable was one of her specially saving graces. I think she was amused when she took what I knew were her last breaths, and I chose to sing her favourite hymn to her: "Lead Kindly Light amidst the Encircling Gloo-hoom." "Why not I dre-hemt I dwe-helt in mar-harble halls?" she would have asked if she had the breath, the song that echoed round all her houses. She had a pretty voice, and with her dramatic gifts would have made a success on the stage if that had been an option. Of course like all the girls of her class and time she had few options, so she had to create richness, thrills, magic out of the humdrum, invent a long running drama in which we her family must take bit parts. As her only daughter I was to be beautiful and docile, a source of pride but not a threat. In fact I was dumpy and disabled with polio from the age of nine months, my right leg failing to develop. It was a situation neither of us came to terms with, her disappointment, my guilt, like a grey haze around us till the end.

She left letters, photographs, albums, diaries, and from them I was able to fill in some of the gaps in her story. I wanted to discover especially what effect the East had on the Joneses. Since my great grandmother Maria had gone to India as a bride in 1851 three generations of women in the family had spent most of their lives there. In the process three generations of children had been separated very young from their parents, in the care of relatives or in Holiday homes. It seems bizarre now, it was accepted as normal then. What did it do to the children? To my mother, to me, to my family? I didn't think I would find all the answers, and even when I knew them would it lift the burden of guilt I carried, a burden shared by all the women whose husbands chose to be empire builders. The White Woman's Burden, of which Kipling never sang, was perhaps the hardest of all to bear.

Introduction by Susan Bayly[3]

Iris Macfarlane's son, Professor Alan Macfarlane, comments on the hundred-year period when four generations of her family's women lived as white memsahibs in British India:

'It was an extraordinary moment in history, when a small band of middle class ladies held together the greatest Empire on earth, to their private cost and pain.'

In the ever-growing academic literature on the experiences and legacies of empire, it is now widely accepted that the intimacies of colonial domestic life did indeed play a critical role in both the making and unmaking of the Western colonisers' power. [4] Across a wide range of colonised societies in both hemispheres, nineteenth- and twentieth-century commentators frequently used the metaphor of the Western *bourgeois* family as a means of defending and legitimating colonial rule. Much that was said and done in colonial settings rested on conceptions which represented the empire's schools, regiments and other key institutions as family-like in nature.

In Iris's richly peopled memoir of her maternal family the Joneses and of her own childhood and married life, the British tea firm director uttering words of patronising praise for the 'company wives' who braved India's fleeting 1962 Chinese invasion panic is only one of the many old colonial hands who thought in these terms. [5] Those who spoke on behalf of these corporate entities, and indeed the empires themselves, often characterised them as moral units which endured through time. Of course these attitudes held sway in many other settings too in the age of the nineteenth- and twentieth-century Raj. Indeed they are still alive today in both Western and non-Western societies, even in institutions

---

[3] Reader in Historical Anthropology at the University of Cambridge
[4] Key works on these issues include: Strobel, M. and N. Chaudhuri (eds.) 1992 *Western Women and Imperialism. Complicity and resistance*. Bloomington: Indiana University Press; McClintock, A. 1995 *Imperial leather: race, gender, and sexuality in the colonial context*. London: Routledge; Cooper, F. and A. Stoler (eds.) 1997 *Tensions Of Empire*. Berkeley: University California Press; Clancy-Smith, J. & F. Gouda (eds.) 1998 *Domesticating The Empire: Race, Gender, & Family Life In French & Dutch Colonialism*. Charlottesville: University of Virginia; Burton, A. (ed.). 1999 *Gender, Sexuality & Colonial Modernities* London: Routledge; Stoler, A. 2002 *Carnal knowledge & imperial power* Berkeley: University of California.
[5] This anecdote is all the more interesting in showing that the big British tea firms were still being run on a basis of recognisably colonial race and gender relations nearly 20 years after Independence. Iris and her son, my senior colleague Professor Alan Macfarlane, have documented these and other aspects of this old and troubled global industry in their brilliant book *Green Gold. The empire of tea* 2003 (Ebury)

which are widely thought of as embodiments of ultra-modern and hence impersonal economic and social norms.

Thus the idea of the boss or commanding officer as father, and of the firm, regiment, school or nation as a family with rights of governance over the morals and conduct of those within its embrace, was never an exclusively colonial phenomenon. But as Iris makes poignantly clear in her evocations of the claims of regimental, school and national spirit, colonial versions of these demands and moralities could be particularly hard to bear. Like real families both within and beyond the colonial empires, regiments and other familial organisations, including big commercial companies as well as public bodies, could be visualised as webs of inheritable solidarities which rested to a very considerable degree on the moral and bodily dispositions of women. Thus they had both a legal and affective or emotional life, imparting identity as well as nurture to those who shared their bonds of membership.

What these family-like units required in return was that those whom they called their own showed respect for regimental or company hierarchies, and strove at all times to defend and identify with their interests. And as Iris's account so vividly conveys, it was in this regard that the pains and absurdities of colonial life could be most keenly felt by the wives and daughters of empire. Iris herself experienced the compelling force of the empire-as-family idea in many ways and settings. One notable manifestation of its demands was in India during the Second World War, when the officers senior to her temporary soldier husband – in peacetime an Assam tea planter - made her painfully aware that she was a deficient and unwifely adopted daughter of the regiment. Her crime, like so much else in the book recalled by Iris with an unflinching eye for the absurdities and casual brutalities of the white expatriate's world, was that she had resisted her contemporaries' definitions of the duties of an officer's wife.

Interestingly enough, this loving, dedicated, careerless mother had earned opprobrium for both her husband and herself by treating the claims of her own home and children as her paramount concern. By the standards of the time and place – a colonial outpost, full of white Britons who were fearfully aware of the need to rely on potentially disaffected Asian troops as a bulwark against the terrifying Japanese military machine – Iris had behaved badly. To these censorious officers and their wives, she had failed to defer to the needs of her wider imperial family unit, her husband's regiment, by resisting both its implied and explicit calls to spend her days in pointless volunteer 'war work'.[6]

---

[6] 'War work' for women in blitz-ravaged Britain was a widely acknowledged moral duty, part of the pulling together required of all on the 'home front' regardless of class or gender in the desperate days of 'people's war' against Hitler. Doing 'war work' in India and thus going against the grain of memsahib convention was clearly for some a conscience-salving exercise: despite the fear of Japanese invasion, throughout the war the whites in India and other overseas colonies not under Japanese occupation were widely held to be safe and privileged compared to their fellow citizens at 'home'.

It is notable that this was not responsible or challenging work like that performed by the women in uniform whom Iris remembers seeing in those wartime cantonment towns. As with much else recounted here, this reflected the narrow and on occasion astoundingly heartless upbringing experienced by all the Jones women whose lives Iris explores so evocatively. The callousness of her forebears' treatment of their children – especially mothers' treatment of daughters – comes across to a present-day reader as almost unimaginable. Far from being nurtured and cossetted as a child with an able mind and a serious physical disability, Iris was made to feel defective and inferior for failing to possess the physical attractiveness and hardy physique expected of a Jones daughter.

These are attitudes that I have encountered too. Within my own marital family, I have heard similar stories from one of the many Englishwomen – an octogenarian whose keen intelligence and vitality are reminiscent of Iris's - whose girlhood was blighted by the eugenicist thinking of the 1920s. One of the prevailing tenets of those times was that short-sightedness was a sign of inherited mental and physical deficiency, and possible 'feeble-mindedness'. This was not a Raj service family like Iris's: it is not all that long ago that such attitudes were held to be both scientific and progressive, and they were certainly not specific to 'imperial' environments. [7]

*

In Iris's case, it is almost unbearable to read that her family nickname was Jane, short for 'Plain Jane', and that her face was obliterated from pictures in a family photo album: this for a child who was condemned for many years to the wearing of hideous and painful leg-irons, in a futile attempt to correct her disability. Just as heartrending is the account of a small Victorian Jones, the last in her family to be sent to a grim boarding school in India, rather than an equally dismal establishment at 'home' in Scotland or England. Iris reproduces a horrible letter telling this unhappy child that she would receive no more mail from the family until she ceased to afflict them with her accounts of misery at the school in which she was experiencing torments of homesickness.

What these and many other vignettes in the book show very clearly is that like other middle class Britons of the nineteenth and early twentieth centuries, Joneses manifested their fervent Christian piety in cultic outpourings of grief when their children died of the many sicknesses that decimated Raj families. But when alive, their offspring had no right to complain, demand or otherwise fall below the family's exacting standards of discipline and filial duty.

The enduring force of Jones racism is another family trait dealt with by Iris with devastating precision. She is notably frank and self-critical about the slow

---

[7] See Dikotter, F., 1998 'Race Culture: Recent Perspectives on the History of Eugenics' *The American Historical Review*, 103, 2 pp. 467-478.

transition that she herself made from an unthinking sense of distance and superiority in her attitude to Indians. And she throws considerable light on her forebears' obsessive concerns with racial 'otherness'.

This too was as much about domestic as specifically colonial forms of difference. As in the case of so many others of their class and worldview, Jewishness was as repugnant to her Jones forebears as the 'stain' of mixed-race descent, though – in the hideous language of the day - it was any perceived 'touch of the tarbrush' that truly disqualified potential suitors for a Jones daughter. Thus one of the other messages conveyed in parental admonitions to that same homesick nineteenth-century Jones child was that she must take pains to avoid the contaminating touch of any dark-skinned mixed-race child or adult, and to spurn such persons if they sought to befriend her. Indeed among the key reasons for exiling the white children of the Raj to those far-away British schools was the fear of precisely such entanglements with the world of the '*deshi*', the 'native-born', including – often especially - those born of mixed-race unions. *Deshi* mores, accents, diseases and other communicable influences and embodied threats were widely said to be among the greatest social and physical perils of the 'orient'. [8]

As Iris's unrepentant mother also made plain when she revealed in old age that she had quietly sabotaged her clever daughter's chances of an Oxford scholarship, Jones women were not to aspire to careers or higher education. And especially while young, their personal tastes and yearnings were of no account in the higher scheme of family goals and career strategies. So at their icy English and Scottish boarding schools, and in the homes of the reluctant kin and strangers' families where they lodged in the absence of their far-away parents, they were groomed for early marriage to a man with the white skin and solid career prospects deemed suitable for a Jones girl. The terms of this suitability seem to have stayed remarkably constant in the course of the change-filled century which her narrative brings so vividly to life.

Iris's understated yet devastating explorations of these matters make one recognise that like individuals, families differ, and that over-broad generalisations about empire-builders are as dangerous and undesirable as any other kind of racial or cultural stereotyping, whether propounded by racist Victorians or modern-day academics. What readers thus learn from Iris's account of her family's hatred of brainy female 'blue-stockings', and their undisguised revulsion at her supposed unprettiness and physical disability – a withered leg caused by the infant polio attack which her parents had failed to notice or take seriously at

---

[8] See Stoler 2002, and compare White, O. 1999 *Children of the French empire: miscegenation and colonial society in French West Africa, 1895-1960* New York: Oxford University Press. See also Daunton, M. and R. Halpern (eds.) 1999 *Empire and Others. British encounters with indigenous peoples, 1600-1850*. Philadelphia: University of Pennsylvania.

the time - is that the narrow conventions of her family ruled out for her the many things — including university and career fulfilment — that had become possible even for some of the daughters of empire by the years of her girlhood and early married life. For others, but not for Iris, this expansion of women's opportunities was particularly dramatic in wartime, when even the most conservative defenders of colonial power and 'white prestige' found their assumptions about race, class and gender being rapidly undermined.

*

As for Iris's bad behaviour as a wartime officer's wife, she was made to feel small on yet another occasion when, pregnant and queasy, she failed in her duty of enthusiastic attendance at one of the regiment's bloody public soldier's rituals. These time-honoured regimental activities, involving the sacrificial slaughter of buffaloes as the officers and their memsahibs looked on and applauded, were held to play an essential role in securing the loyalty of 'native' troops.

Here we catch a glimpse of the most enduring anxieties of the coloniser's world. Iris had been brought up on what turns out to have been the heavily romanticised family legend of her great grandmother, together with her doctor great grandfather and their children, narrowly escaping death at the hands of insurgent colonial troops in the great 1857 rebellion. This event, which Indians refer to as the first Independence War, and which traumatised Britons called the Mutiny, began in a regiment of north Indian sepoys (soldiers), though it rapidly spread to the wider peasant and urban populace of the Gangetic plain. This turning point in the history of the Raj came to be widely seen as a response to the clumsy handling by white Christian officers of a host of issues to do with their soldiers' sensitivities in matters of religion and cherished social distinction. [9]

The Mutiny background is of considerable relevance to the raucous rite at which Iris found it so difficult to display the requisite *sang-froid* in a critical hour of imperial need. Even if they did not draw an explicit parallel with that earlier crisis of empire, the regiment's commanders clearly thought it vital to transmit something very different from the message the sepoys had received from their cack-handed East India Company officers in 1857.

These soldiers of 1941 had to be told repeatedly and emphatically about the high esteem in which they were held. There was nothing trivial about this exercise. At the end of the war, Iris's husband shed tears of distress when he was required to attend the execution of some of the thousands of Indian men and women who had joined the Indian National Army, a force raised by the radical

---

[9] Stokes, E. 1986 (C. A. Bayly, ed.) *The peasant armed. The Indian revolt of 1857*. Oxford: Clarendon; Roy, T 1996 *The politics of a popular uprising. Bundelkhand in 1857* Delhi: Oxford University Press; Alavi, S. 1998 *The sepoys and the Company: tradition and transition in Northern India, 1770-1830*. Delhi, Oxford: University Press; G Bhadra 'Four rebels of 1857', in Guha, R and G. Spivak (eds) 1988 *Selected Subaltern Studies* Oxford: University Press.

nationalist leader Subhas Chandra Bose to fight on the Japanese side against Britain's King-Emperor. Nowadays its members are revered by many as Indian national heroes. Those of its recruits who were hanged as traitors by the British are hailed as martyrs of the anti-colonial freedom struggle, that is as lost sons and daughters of yet another kin group, the family of the Indian national homeland, which is often represented as a nurturing motherland in both past and contemporary Indian political iconography.[10]

So on that dusty cantonment parade ground in 1941, what was taking place was a determined attempt to drive home the point that the still 'loyal' troops of her husband's regiment were subordinate but cherished members of the empire's white-ruled family. This required the presence of all the family's members — including pregnant young temporary officers' wives — at occasions like this one at which the Hindu soldiers' traditions of faith and heritage were being publicly honoured. It was therefore made plain to Iris that as a dutiful imperial wife and daughter, her schooling and background should have equipped her to master any fears or infirmities rendering her unfit to take her place in this show of familial solidarity.

These notions of regimental duty and identity were part of a much wider set of ideas and images through which white colonisers from all the imperial nation states sought to impose order and meaning on the perplexing realities of their overseas dominions. It is very striking, however, that the white people with whom Iris and her forebears lived come across in the book as knowing or at least caring very little about the vast array of detailed statistical, analytical and descriptive writings which the empires' officials produced so tirelessly in the attempt to count, tax, police and 'civilise' their subjects.

To present-day scholars for whom rulership in general and colonial statecraft in particular were above all an exercise in data-collection and 'power-knowledge', this great nineteenth- and twentieth-century enterprise of colonial information-seeking was a critical prop of every imperial system. According to a multitude of recent academic studies, it was through the interpretation of these census statistics and ethnographic materials - rather than more overt manifestations of colonial power – that white colonisers constructed new lived realities for their Asian and other subjects. Through 'power-knowledge', say these historians and colonial culture theorists, colonisers conceived and brought into being an India of supposedly ineradicable caste and religious divisions, and an Africa of

---

[10] See Ghosh, K.K. 1969, *The Indian National Army. Second Front of the Indian national movement* Meerut; Gordon, L. 1990 *Brothers against the Raj. A biography of Indian nationalists, Sarat and Subhas Chandra Bose* New York: Columbia University; Fay, P. W. 1994 *The forgotten army. India's armed struggle for Independence, 1942-45* Ann Arbor: University of Michigan.

primordial 'tribalism', doing so through the creation and strategic deployment of invented and self-serving statistical and ethnographic categories. [11]

The strikingly different picture that comes across in Iris's account may surprise those who have been inclined to exaggerate or oversimplify the effects of this power-knowledge phenomenon, particularly those who see it as a one-way traffic in which the colonised had no voice or power. [12] So it is important and salutary to be reminded of what *Daughters of Empire* demonstrates so effectively. This is that despite their moments of both largescale and personal catastrophe, in the routinised and domesticated worlds of tea and cantonment, the white Britons in middling managerial, administrative and professional positions tended to lead bookless, humdrum lives. Few apparently felt much, if any, hunger for knowledge of their non-white subjects' languages, cultures, histories and inner lives. Against this background of incuriosity, Iris's battles to learn local languages and to lead an intellectually and emotionally fulfilling life as a planter's wife, engaging with the rich cultural world around her, becoming a published author, and seeking to improve both health care and schooling for her husband's tea workers, are truly remarkable.

*

There is a further point to make about that relentlessly uninformed environment of the planting and soldiering expatriates, in which her contemporaries' notions of how to live among the people who worked or soldiered for them seem to have been shaped only very indirectly by the complex and elaborate 'readings' of Indian life to which present-day scholars give so much emphasis. What is evident from her account is that expatriates like the ones we meet in the book operated both in relation to one another, and to their subjects, on the basis of ideas that were often far simpler than those that are now widely said to have pervaded the 'colonial mind'. The colonial thinking that Iris documents reflects a flatter and duller account of the 'oriental' world. Her fellow Britons' 'idea of India' comes across as a web of familiar rather than exotic social units, that is as an arena of family hierarchies and crudely conceived racial differences, rather than one more particularistically defined by the ties of caste, religion, tribe, culture and alien civilisational norms.

These 'orientalist' classifications, and the parallel ideas which were generated in subject territories beyond the subcontinent, were undoubtedly important to other, more formalised understandings of colonised societies. But they were clearly not central to the everyday thinking of Iris's contemporaries, and that of her family's generations of modestly educated middle class men and women.

---

[11] See e.g. Cohn, B. 1998 *Colonialism and its Forms of Knowledge: the British in India* Princeton.
[12] A view challenged in Bayly, C.A. 1996 *Empire and information: Intelligence gathering and social communication in India, 1780–1870*. Cambridge: University Press

The empire-as-family idea also played out on a wider stage than that of the workaday world of the Joneses and their fellow planters and middle-rank soldiers and professionals. Both in its nineteenth-century heyday, and in the decades of colonialism's fraught and painful twentieth-century decline, conservative as well as liberal observers represented their empires' Asian and African subjects as weak-willed women or wilful children, in need of the guiding hand of a rational and authoritative male protector and patriarch. And insofar as they could tell such people as their client princes, Christian converts or plantation workers how to lead their lives, missionaries and modern-minded administrators held up an image of their own idealised home life as a pattern of perfection for those who experienced Western rule.[13]

This imagined ideal took the form of a monogamous, propertied conjugal unit, living respectably, piously, hygienically, and productively. It was a stereotype which embodied all the material and moral virtues which the coloniser's superior civilisation and capitalist economic order were supposed to be imparting, at least to the more deserving and 'evolved' of their non-white subjects. Towards virtually everyone else of course, including ordinary 'native' tillers and tribesmen, and the small but vocal and increasingly politicised colonial *intelligentsia*s, there were the indifferent and sometimes venomously racist attitudes which are recalled with such bitterness by many of the empires' former subjects.

Among those with the worst of these memories are those who experienced such horrors as British officialdom's uncaring response to the 1943 Bengal Famine, or the pains that were taken to succour the fleeing white but not Indian expatriates during the hellish flight through Burma of the millions seeking escape from the invading Japanese army in 1942.[14] In the chapters on her own early married years, Iris's pitilessly self-critical older self characterises these attitudes as having underpinned many of the assumptions and blindnesses of her own baffled, decent, struggling, but often hopelessly blundering younger self.

She brings to life just such a moment in her account of one of her epic wartime railway journeys. She was 19, a year into her marriage to Mac the tea planter. Exhausted and dehydrated, she helplessly allows herself – travelling on her own with a kitten, no food or drink, and her infant first-born son - to close her ears to the pleas of desperate Indians seeking entry into the safety of her half-empty railway compartment, shared with an odious fellow memsahib, as she too flees from the Assam tea gardens in the face of the incoming Japanese onslaught.

---

[13] Comaroff, J. & J. Comaroff, 1991 *Of revelation and revolution: Christianity, colonialism, and consciousness in South Africa.* Chicago: University Press; Comaroff, J. 1997. 'Images of empire, contests of conscience' in Cooper, F. & A. Stoler (eds.), *Tensions Of Empire* Berkeley: University of California.

[14] Bayly, C. and T. Harper 2004 *Forgotten armies The fall of British Asia, 1941-1954* London: Allen Lane.

Inevitably, then, the stereotype of the idealised Western home aroused a host of anxieties, tensions, dilemmas and conflicts at the level of lived reality, both for colonisers and their subjects. These were often most painful for the kinds of people whose lives were vividly evoked by novelists like Kipling, Maugham, John Masters and Paul Scott – and more melodramatically, by the makers of atmospheric 1930s films like *Shanghai Express, Rain*, and *The Letter*. These too are stories set in exoticised tropical locations. In all of them, the great screen stars of the day portray dangerous, suffering women who fall foul of the suffocating conventions enunciated by narrow-minded planters, churchmen, blimpish soldiers, and other male establishment figures.

In my own early fieldwork days in India in the 1970s, I came across a family whose story could easily have been turned into one of those steamy, suggestive Hollywood film plots. Their nineteenth-century bungalow was shared by the elderly widowed white wife and Eurasian daughter of a British coffee planter. The younger woman was the planter's daughter by his Indian mistress. She had the education and skills which her memsahib stepmother lacked, and it was this younger woman who ran the plantation.

The two were locked in a grim, silent battle over the terms of the planter's will. The gloomy house with its breathtaking hill views quivered with the unvoiced rage that had been festering between them since the planter's death 20 years earlier. Their situation was further complicated by the militancy of their now unionised estate workers, and the fear that the regional government was about to nationalise the plantations. These were now of course an uncomfortable legacy of the economic and social order of the pre-Independence period. The younger woman spoke resignedly of emigration. Other Eurasians I knew in the same region also found post-Independence India a difficult and hostile place. Some were actively seeking immigrant visas for countries they considered more congenial. These were invariably the 'white' lands of the former empire, Australia and Canada.

The significance of such people's experiences is now of great interest to the many historians of empire who have turned away from issues of high politics, macro-level economic change and grand strategies. Often in alliance with anthropologists, such scholars have focused on the discovery of 'subaltern' (non-elite) histories. Their works seek to understand the everyday and the experiential in the lives of women, children, domestic servants, so-called poor whites, and other people on the margins of 'respectable' colonial society, including the children of white fathers and their quasi-permanent 'native' sexual partners. [15]

---

[15] See works cited in note 1; also Stoler, A. 1992 'Constructing Local Boundaries. Sexual Affronts and Racial Frontiers: European Identities and the Cultural Politics of Exclusion in Colonial Southeast Asia' *Comparative Studies in Society and History*, 34, 3 pp. 514-551

*

Iris's account provides many insights into the diversity and pathos of those worlds, her own memories movingly enriched and contextualised by her use of her family's remarkable treasure trove of letters and diaries. The teenage British soldier's wife whose baby dies, and who then becomes a temporary wet-nurse to the more privileged Victorian memsahib's newborn child, is only one of the many individuals whose own painfully vulnerable family lives intersected with those of the Jones women. Sometimes these intersections occurred harmoniously, and sometimes at great cost to all concerned. Those who bore the brunt were often the young mothers who were confronted daily with the fear of the diseases and mysterious, half-articulated moral dangers of the 'tropics' that they were somehow to keep at bay from within the fragile shelter of their bungalows and first-class railway carriages.

For the colonised too, especially in India, images and idealisations of domesticity loomed very large in the concerns of those who both lived and contested the social and political inequalities of the Raj. By the end of the First World War, as the claims of empire came under fire from within and beyond Britain's colonies and dominions, anti-colonial nationalists framed their challenges to imperial authority in terms which focused both painfully and passionately on the arena of the family and the marital home. Many of these exhortations placed their emphasis on calls for reform and 'uplift' in the conduct, decorum and education of the wives and daughters of the nation's future citizens. [16]

Such concerns were particularly strong in cases such as India's, in which vilification of 'native' marital and childcare practices had long featured in the writings of Western and non-Western public moralists. A case in point was the outrage felt by Gandhi and other Indian nationalists at the publication in 1927, five years after Iris's birth, of the American journalist Katherine Mayo's sensationalising book *Mother India*. This luridly 'orientalist' polemic represented Indian home life as unhealthy, unhygienic, and eroticised to the point of depravity, arguing on this basis that Indians were unfit for '*swaraj*' (self rule, i.e. independence from colonial suzerainty). [17]

---

[16] Chatterjee, P., 1990 'The Nationalist Resolution of the Women's Question', in Sangari, K. and S. Vaid (eds.) *Recasting Women. Essays in Indian Colonial History.* New Brunswick: Rutgers University Press, pp.233-253; Burton, A. 1998 'From Child Bride to "Hindoo Lady": Rukhmabai and the Debate on Sexual Respectability in Imperial Britain' *The American Historical Review*, 103, 4, pp. 1119-1146.

[17] Said, E., 1979. *Orientalism: Western Conceptions of the Orient*, New York: Vintage. And see Mayo, K. 2000 *Mother India. Selections from the Controversial 1927 Text* (Mrinalini Sinha, ed..) Ann Arbor: University of Michigan.

When families like Iris's repressed their children's longings, and sought to ward off contacts and influences that might inflame or corrupt their wills and appetites, they were 'othering' a host of things and human types originating in places both remote and close to home. Thus in the narrow, philistine schooling that they sought for their children, and in their reluctance to praise or indulge them, many fearful parents had in mind an array of counter-models deriving from both colonial and domestic sources. These were the visions of 'promiscuous' or 'degraded' home life presented as a cautionary tale by Mayo. But they were prefigured in innumerable other nineteenth- and twentieth-century accounts of the many physical and moral dangers threatening the decency and stability that right-minded people were called upon to create and sustain in familial settings. [18]

As far as the colonial world is concerned, it has been widely observed that in the late nineteenth and twentieth centuries, men's rather than women's voices and concerns generally defined and steered both Indian and British debates about colonial domestic life. It is no longer common to find either Indian or Western historians celebrating the subcontinent's modernising nationalists as liberators of oppressed Indian women. Many scholars now seek to expose and 'deconstruct' the male preoccupations and anxieties that they see as having underpinned the calls for female education and 'uplift' made by the leaders of colonial Asia's great mass nationalist movements, and particularly by the key figures of the Indian National Congress. These campaigns have come to be routinely seen as attempts to gratify male needs by turning the Indian domestic arena into a nurturing shelter for those suffering from the psychic wounds inflicted by the coloniser. [19]

Thus even if literate and equipped with suitable 'modern' skills and knowledge, the nation's educated mothers, wives and sisters were to be helpmeets rather than independent agents, their only goal to devote themselves to the creation of a warm, secure redoubt for the beleaguered men who struggled to find dignity and fulfilment in the colonial public arena. Far from being truly emancipated, such women have come to be thought of as merely burdened with new and demanding expectations in this battle to turn first the private household, and then the whole ancestral homeland, into a zone of freedom and self-empowering mastery for the colonial authorities' male heirs and successors.

---

[18] On the moralising literature that drew on both 'native' and European sources in instructing Indian householders about the need for 'purity' in the domestic arena, see Walsh J., 2004 *Domesticity in colonial India.* Lanham: Rowman and Littlefield. And see also Davidoff, L. and C. Hall, (eds.) 1987 *Family fortunes. Men and women of the English middle class, 1780 – 1850* London: Routledge; and
Ram K. and M. Jolly (eds) 1998 *Maternities and modernities. Colonial and postcolonial experiences in Asia and the Pacific.* Cambridge: University Press.
[19] Nandy, A. 1989 *The intimate enemy. Loss and recovery of self under colonialism.* Oxford: University Press.

Many of the most influential works on these aspects of colonialism have therefore focused on the so-called colonial 'woman question' as a conundrum of self-diagnosis that was generally framed, posed, and responded to by authoritative men. Its central premise was thus the problem of 'recapturing' forms of dignity and autonomy that were represented by many Indian commentators and other colonial intellectuals as something to achieve through acts of self-assertion which restored the lost or damaged masculinity of the colonised nation's male populace. To be master of a proper home was to be on the road to mastery of one's freed and recaptured nation. So these were often debates and polemical programmes in which colonised women too were spoken of and to about their duties and deficiencies, rather than having the scope to become active agents, or to be acknowledged as such by those who sought to reform, protect, 'advance' or restrict them. [20]

It is widely said too that these problematic views and attitudes were part of a broader complex of pathologised colonial experiences which have had an enduring afterlife. Their effects may still be discerned among the descendants of both white and non-white participants in the troubled lives of empires. And the pernicious consequences of colonialism are held to be particularly visible today in the pains and unresolved psychic and social traumas of the 'postcolonial predicament' [21] These after-effects of empire have been documented both in studies of the turbulent nation states of the former colonial world, and in accounts of their manifestations in the fraught interactions and traffickings between metropoles and ex-colonies, as enacted by people, products and less tangible connections and cultural 'flows'. [22]

It is certainly provocative and stimulating to contemplate this growing literature on the troubled legacies of empire. Yet it is problematic too that so much of what has been said about both the former colonies and their ex-rulers represents most or all that shaped the experiences of these people and places as a matter of narrowly defined colonial interactions.

I am certainly not calling for the whitewashing or romanticising of the empires and their afterlives. And there is nothing in Iris's penetrating and unsentimental evocation of her own experiences and those of her family that could possibly be seen as an exercise in Raj nostalgia, or as complacent self-congratulation of the

---

[20] Chatterjee, P. 1993 The *nation and its fragments*. Princeton: University Press; Chakrabarty, D. 1994 'The difference-deferral of colonial modernity' in Arnold, D. & D. Hardiman (eds.) *Subaltern studies* vol 8, Oxford: University Press.
[21] Breckenridge, C. and P. van der Veer (eds.) 1993 *Orientalism and the postcolonial predicament. Perspectives on south Asia.* Philadelphia: University of Pennsylvania.
[22] Appadurai, A. 1996 *Modernity at large. Cultural dimensions of globalisation* Minneapolis: University of Minnesota

kind to be found in a different set of recent writings: those seeking to rehabilitate and glorify the heritage of the colonising empires. [23]

Yet one of the striking features of Iris's memoir is the extent to which it reveals the highly segmented worlds in which memsahibs from families like hers lived their lives as daughters of empire. The world of the nineteenth- and twentieth-century Joneses emerges here as one in which expatriates did not really live to any significant degree in the kind of poisonous intimacy with non-white people that is now regularly cited as a defining feature of the colonial environment. The presence of the white expatriates certainly had a profound and enduring impact on India. But its effects were more often felt at a distance than through the continual intersections and obsessive imaginings that many commentators have focused on in their accounts of colonialism's sexual and moral encounters.

The problem with all but the most sophisticated 'intimate enemy' perspectives is that they tend to overlook the extent to which colonisers and colonised so often lived in very separate worlds, taking far less notice of one another than one might expect from current writings on the painful psychodynamics of colonial life. One reason for this is the tendency to rely on literary texts as a guide to colonial life and thought. Sophisticated works like Ann Stoler's, which draw instead on ethnographic and archival evidence to explore the cultures and moralities of the colonial world, offer more nuanced and convincing insights into the lived experiences of both the sons and daughters of empire. Iris's narrative is based on careful and imaginative exploration of comparable sources: her own memories, and that rich and compelling collection of family papers. She too is therefore a more reliable guide to the intimacies of imperial family life than many of the academics who make sweeping claims about colonial cultures and their psychic effects through analysis of novels and film scripts.

What I have in mind here about the limitations and real if leaky boundaries separating white and non-white people is not just a matter of that prevailing philistine indifference to place, people and culture which I have already referred to as a characteristic of the Raj environments which Iris describes. Throughout the age of empire, there certainly were officials and other expatriates who were unlike the workaday people we meet in Iris's account. In Assam as in other colonial settings, many Britons did seek to 'civilise', Christianise, or otherwise change and 'uplift' their colonial subjects. For such people, colonial life was imbued with purpose and ideological commitment, however crudely, haphazardly or harmfully they conceived and acted upon these goals and ideals.

Yet we miss out on something equally important about the ways in which empire shaped the lives and minds of both colonisers and the colonised by disregarding the very different perceptions and dispositions which large numbers of other expatriates brought to the lands in which they sought their livelihoods.

---

[23] Ferguson, N. 2002 *Empire .The rise and demise of the British world order and the lessons for global power* London: Allen Lane

For Iris's male and female forebears, India was not a cause but an instrument. In this it resembled Nigeria and other zones of so-called indirect rule in sub-Saharan Africa. In these colonies, too, most whites lived as birds of passage, generally retiring 'home' to Britain on retirement or widowhood. They were thus very different from the places in which expatriates created property-owning settler societies; the emigrants who colonised Australia and the other anglophone 'white dominions' constituted themselves on a very different basis, one of citizenry rather than career-based cadreship. [24]

What this meant of course was that India was never 'home' for families like Iris's. For men, it was primarily a source of secure if unexalted employment. For women, it was a place to be taken or sent by their parents on leaving school in order to make respectable marriages. In this, as Iris explains, as a shy, unpolished teenager she was following a path already well trodden by her mother and other female forebears. And while this process has been recounted in many other memoirs and novels of Raj life, she is both moving and entertaining in evoking the anxieties and embarrassments of the sweaty club socials at which she was expected to parade as a potential match for one of the bride-seeking bachelor planters or civil servants with whom she clumped unhappily around the dance floor. [25]

Here too, Iris points to something that was very general for middle-class Britons, rather than being specific to the colonial world. For all but the most exceptional families or individuals, a woman who failed to achieve marriage to an acceptable partner – white, middle class, British, with adequate career prospects – had only the grimmest of alternatives before her. This was a matter of economic circumstances as much as moral and social constraints. Though its elder women were apparently often terrifyingly fierce in defence of now-forgotten standards of refinement in dress and manners, Iris's family were far from rich. When unmarried, their women certainly lacked the means to sustain independent households, even if any of them had possessed the inclination to challenge convention by doing so. And she and her other female kin were clearly debarred by family convention as well as lack of suitable education to look to teaching or other conventional 'female' careers as an alternative to marriage. Millions of British women solved the problem of impecunious spinsterhood through unskilled wage labour, but of course there could be no question of factory work or domestic service for a woman of Iris's non-elite but still emphatically non-working-class background.

---

[24] Woolfe, P. 1999 *Settler colonialism and the transformation of anthropology* London: Cassell.

[25] See Sinha, M. 2001 'Britishness, Clubbability, and the Colonial Public Sphere: The Genealogy of an Imperial Institution in Colonial India' *The Journal of British Studies*, 40, 4, pp. 489-521.

It is striking that in Iris's world, a financially secure widow could live a life of modest pleasure and self-gratification in the genteel Scottish and English towns and villages which were the true home places of the Joneses and Macfarlanes. But even in Iris's day, an unmarried daughter was condemned to live out her life in such places as that most unenviable of creatures, a stay-at-home unwaged carer for demanding and unaffectionate parents and other kin. And as Iris shows, whether at 'home' or sent out to find a match in India, a young woman's shelf-life in the marriage market was painfully short: hence the grim calculations that she recalls from her own experiences, and which she spots in the letters and diaries of her elder kin, the issue being whether to settle for an aged or otherwise less than ideal husband for a woman growing increasingly anxious about her marital prospects.

This in Iris's family had become a set of problems to be solved in India. The mid-Victorian Joneses had paved the way, and a pragmatic and unsentimental family tradition was thereby created and sustained by the subsequent generations whose members turned to India's or Burma's expatriate planter world when it came time to seek a safe career and a choice of acceptable if unglamorous suitors for their daughters.

In all this there can be no doubt that the Joneses had all the hallmarks of one of the most distinctive institutions of the British empire: the imperial family, as described with penetration and insight by Elizabeth Buettner (2004) [26] But what Iris conveys so compellingly about these unadventurous, salary-seeking service lineages is that they tended both individually and collectively to see themselves in very pragmatic terms.

Certainly the Joneses did not appear to have a sense of family tradition idealising their role as hereditary servants of the Raj and defenders of a great imperial enterprise. What they had to a far greater degree than any vision of themselves as sharers in the noble tasks of empire was a sense of being members of families with obligations to meet as Joneses or Macfarlanes. This meant an obligation to stay solvent if possible, though it is striking to observe how shaky the finances of individual Jones households often were, and how regularly their reluctant relations had to come to the rescue of unlucky or improvident kin. Being a Jones also required conformity to the demands of those other family-like institutions which gave Jones men their careers and livelihoods. This strong sense of one's own family and of the family-like nature of the institutions which provided education and – above all - occupations for oneself and one's close kin defined the duties that family members owed to one another, however reluctantly and unamiably they interacted in the domestic arenas of those convention-loving everyday lives.

---

[26] *Empire Families: Britons and Late Imperial India* Oxford: Oxford University Press.

The lives led by women in those imperial families emerge from Iris's account as full of intense if unpremeditated cruelties. Among these were the painful separations which they imposed on their children. [27]

As Iris shows, the insistence on despatching children to those far-away schools and guardians was accepted as a testing but necessary reality for both mothers and their offspring. It is striking to learn that in the parlance of the day, a woman who went 'home' to be with her children was 'selfish' for failing to focus on her primary duty: care and support of her husband. Those who found that their spouses had succumbed to the ever-present sexual temptations of the 'tropics' had only themselves to blame if their marriages foundered and they found themselves alone and impoverished as a result. In the world of the imperial family, men did the business of empire; the business of women was to support their colonising menfolk by creating and sustaining the expatriate households in which infants and toddlers but not their older children had qualified rights of residence.

Thus in the precarious and turbulent world of empire, the white memsahibs did play a central role in maintaining the far-flung webs of belonging and interaction which defined so many important features of colonial life. What comes across very vividly in Iris's account is that though sometimes rewarding – she writes movingly of her delight in the Assamese landscape, and her moments of marital and maternal joy - this could be an exceedingly unhappy way of life for both adults and children. Yet what is not often appreciated about it is something that Iris makes strikingly clear: for much of the time, it was a surprisingly narrow and segmented existence, only intermittently interacting at close range with the 'native' worlds in which it was embedded and yet so strikingly apart.

Its odd, introspective isolation from the wider worlds of Assamese or other 'native' peoples was sometimes ruptured – indeed on occasion very violently so – most notably in wartime, as Iris found so dramatically in her dangerous moments of flight and vulnerability in a Raj grown suddenly turbulent and insecure even for the most privileged of the memsahibs and their children. At other times the imaginations of memsahibs and other expatriates clearly did not feed obsessively or exclusively on the fearful carnalities and psychic menaces of the 'orient'.

---

[27] The famous short story of 1888, 'Baa Baa, Black Sheep', Kipling's account of his sufferings as a Raj child sent 'home' to reside with unfeeling kin, was a widely read indictment of these practices. Iris has fascinating things to say about the thinking of both children and their parents – including herself - for whom there were no conceivable alternatives to this process. Of course its logic was not unique to the colonial world, and indeed was closely related to the nineteenth- and twentieth-century faith in single-sex boarding schools as the sole means by which the minds and characters of both upper middle-class and aristocratic Britons could be forged and protected from the softening influences that were so widely held to make stay-at-home young 'foreigners' weaker and less fit for the tasks of governance both at home and abroad than their British counterparts.

One might think otherwise from the plots of old films and novels. But from source materials like those excavated so tellingly by Iris, the impression created is that even for members of imperial families like the Joneses, the colonised tropics were often rendered humdrum and even virtually irrelevant to the imaginative lives of the white memsahibs and their kin.

This too is something that I have encountered. When I have listened to the reminiscences of octogenarians whose backgrounds were comparable to Iris's, I have found that for these people too, the most powerful and compelling spaces of youthful memory – insofar as these were imagined as a world beyond 'home' - were those of either Europe or the USA and the 'white dominions'. Even for those who had some experience of India through professional service or marriage, what such individuals convey is a sense of segmentation rather than panoptic completeness. Like Iris, those who had experience of the subcontinent tend to recall only the most fleeting contacts with Indians. The Asians with whom they did interact at a somewhat less superficial level were often those who like them were part of the diasporic 'flows' and migratory occupational movements of the modern empire.

A case in point were the Asian seamen serving on merchant navy vessels with people like my late father-in-law. Roy was a retired British mariner who spoke and wrote with eloquence and penetration about his life at sea, plying the transatlantic and Indian Ocean shipping routes in the years of Iris's girlhood and early married days. [28] As soon as he left school, Roy's parents signed him over as a 16-year-old apprentice on a venerable British cargo vessel. His first voyage lasted for two years. As for the many very young domestic servants of the nineteenth and early twentieth centuries, one should not forget that it was not only the children of the empire's planters and Raj officials for whom it was the norm to live lives of protracted separation from home and family.

In that maritime world of empire, the Asian sailors employed by the British shipping lines were known to the whites who officered or worked alongside them only by the time-honoured generic term 'lascar'. [29] They might have been Indians, Malays or even Chinese: Roy did not recall anyone ever asking or being interested, though he spoke of them with respect as skilful sailors who made better workmates than many of his fellow Britons. He was particularly disparaging about rights-conscious, prickly, left-wing Glaswegians, whom he regarded as clannish and devious. The Asian 'lascars' were thus welcome and necessary in this workaday merchant service world. Even so, they were far less fascinating and exotic to the Britons who sailed with them than the white

---

[28] His lively unpublished memoir, completed shortly before his death in 1994 (*Spun Yarns* by R.E. Bayly) has been deposited with the Imperial War Museum.

[29] A word derived originally from a Persian/Urdu word for an arms-bearing recruit or crewman.

urbanites with their glamorous clothes and strangely accented English whom they encountered in port cities like New York, Sydney and Halifax.

There is another treasure trove of family letters, diaries, photographs and amateur film footage in the Cambridge University Centre of South Asian Studies. These materials too provide instructive insights into the minds and feelings of expatriate Britons in the age of empire. And what they too convey is an overwhelming impression of narrowness and segmentation in the lives led by memsahibs and their menfolk.

In many cases, both their writings, and the pictorial record they created in the form of snapshots and home movies, treat the subcontinent as little more than a shadowy backdrop to the routines of the club and bungalow. The excitements they record are gymkhanas and amateur theatricals; their moments of glory occur at pet shows and hunting parties. Those more like Iris, a passionate and creative gardener, lavished their energies on yet another of those enduring colonial pastimes: the making of domestic gardens in tropical settings. So these too were sons and daughters of the Raj who generally responded to India as a vegetative and animal entity rather than a colonised human space, even though the human cost of what they did and thought was a matter of deadly seriousness for those who lived those segmented and imperceptive lives of empire.

*

The exercise of memory is a phenomenon of great interest and debate for present-day historians and anthropologists. Much has also been written about the nature of narrative as both an oral and a literary mode. Whether public or private, elaborately polished or apparently artless and unprofessional, the accounts that people give of their remembered lives are now widely seen as particularly complex expressions of thought and sensibility. As such, say the specialists, people's testimonies or narrated memoirs must arise not so much from the raw materials of past experience, as from the tale-teller's inheritance of particular conventions for the presentation and understanding of things seen, felt or imagined, and also from the conscious and unconscious sense of one's situation in the here and now. In addition, recollections are said to be shaped by a teller's interactions with those for whom the tale is intended or delivered.[30]

Despite the sophistication of such specialist writings, some tend towards a rather static portrayal of memory and its narrative expressions. Such works treat memories as things 'constructed' or received, rather than reflected on and intellectually grappled with in the process of excavating and ordering

---

[30] Works which have contributed to current understandings of these issues include Tonkin, E. 1995 *Narrating our pasts. The social construction of oral history* Cambridge: University Press; Gilsenan, M. 1996. *Lords of the Lebanese marches. Violence and narrative in an Arab society.* London, New York: Tauris; Butalia, U. 1998 *The other side of silence. Voices from the Partition of India.* New Delhi: Penguin; Skultans, V. 1998 *The testimony of lives. Narrative and memory in post-Soviet Latvia* London: Routledge; Pandey, G. 2001 *Remembering Partition. Violence, nationalism and history in India* Cambridge: University Press.

representations of lives lived or imagined. What is therefore very striking about Iris's account is that it comes across as the product of processes that are dynamic and sharply analytical, as well as being rich in understated emotional power. For readers of her incisive, unsentimental prose, the book is an exercise in something that might best be referred to as critical memory, a process involving analytical reflection, rather than just the reception or inhabiting of things or events recalled and responded to.

So this is emphatically not a work of the kind to which one might apply that dismissive epithet 'Raj nostalgia', implying a lazily conservative form of memory which treats the past as a glamorised refuge and diversion, and disregards its legacies for the heirs of those who experienced its pains and unresolved dilemmas. What Iris has achieved is something entirely different and truly notable. Her book is an account of an extremely active undertaking. It is an application of reflective, analytical thought to the personal recollections which she mines with the same keen eye that she applies to the written record of her family's occasionally upbeat but often terrible life and times. As an expression of memory thoughtfully reviewed and interpreted, it is an account that is astute and critical both of Iris herself, and of the wider colonial world in which her family lived and worked. I am extremely glad to have been introduced to these daughters of empire, and to have seen them through the eyes of someone who was once a part of that sad and distinctive world, and who now thinks and writes about it with such panache and acuity.

DAUGHTERS OF THE EMPIRE

GOING BACK: CHRISTMAS 1996

If there is a hell for me it'll be an endless day in a club in the north Indian state of Assam; a day of staring through dazzling dust at men galloping about on polo grounds; of sitting in sterile circles drinking gin with their wives; of bouncing stickily round an unsprung dance floor, clutched to their soggy shirts; of finally being driven home at night by one of them peering woozily over the wheel, tipping old villagers in bullock carts into the ditch.

I spent thirty years on a tea plantation enduring such days and nights, so why do I want to go back to India after a further thirty years away? For now in 1996 in my mid-seventies I'm going back to the country which bored me and made me ill, but which also enchanted me with its moonflowers and enormous arcs of parrots flying down from the hills at dawn, with its smell of smoke and dust and frying gram and marigolds, with its beautiful people I never got to know. Elderly, arthritic, with a bowel that has never recovered from aeons of assaults by amoeba, I fill a trolley and a small back pack and climb onto a Boeing 747 of Qatar airlines, remembering to buy a bottle of Scotch to sip surreptitiously during turbulence.

Tension brings on indigestion and I hiccough from Cairo to Kathmandu, trying to drink water upside down from a glass between my knees. We fly towards the snows as dawn is laying a crimson and apricot scarf along the horizon. The first sight of the Himalayas stops my heart and also my hiccoughs. A lot of tanned tourists in boots and "Free Tibet" tee shirts get on the plane, but we aren't allowed off. The "Kathmandu Times" is handed round, full of dismal tales of unemployment and corruption, belying the glamour of the name. I take a swig of Scotch as we zoom up through jagged mountains and head down India to Calcutta.

We get out into warm air that makes me regret the long-johns I'm still wearing, but as we go through the airport door I forget about everything except beggar women carrying wizened babies, and stray starving dogs. I was expecting them, braced as it were, but this doesn't shield me from the pain. A small crowd is gathered and someone asks if I am Mother Theresa; do I really look that old and saintly?

A man comes up to enquire if I know his cousin who lives in Rosebank, Surrey. He produces a wallet with a photograph of her, rather dim and blurred, and is disappointed I don't recognize it. He is very happy however, because this very day he has heard he is to be employed by the Corporation. He hopes we shall meet again; so friendly, so cheerful, so un-English, I'm reconciled to not being Mother Theresa or recognizing his cousin.

The taxi honks and bangs its way into the city, just avoiding all the other honking taxis, and the buses, dented and rusty as if they had been recently dug up from a tip. A large poster "Welcome to the City of Joy" is suspended above a row of bits of tin and cardboard, the home of the city's less joyful poor. All the way in there are placards advertising insurance, banking, luxury apartments. "Your future is safe with us" they assure the dwellers on pavements beneath them.

Calcutta at once appals me in a way it never did thirty years ago. Had I become immune, or did company cars, whirling me from airport to air-conditioned hotel immure me from its horrors? I used to use words like "vibrant" "exciting" "stimulating" to describe it. Now for the two nights and a day we spend here, I feel sick, angry, frustrated, horrified that people are allowed to live like this. Louise, who is twenty and travelling with me, loves it.

Not all people. We go to stay with retired planter friends of Louise's mother in their cool and spacious flat in Alipur. There are marble floors and pretty rugs and an enormous television with nine channels, which is on all the time. We drink iced gin as it shows a film about hornbills which is a lot more interesting than our conversation about the good old tea plantations. As Indians they stayed on long after we left, but nothing, as they describe it, changed.

I sleep for fourteen hours and wake to the sound of crows cawing. Opposite is a six storied building, crumbling, glassless, with signs of squatter life and thin orange dogs sleeping in the dust outside. It was bought some years ago to be converted into flats, but money or energy ran out. Next to it is a slightly less battered building festooned with drying clothes. A man sits on a balcony combing his hair, and then peering to see what he has captured in his comb.

It is Sunday and our hosts are going to the Club to play golf, swim, take the grandchildren for pony rides. They have other guests coming, so we have to move on. On the way we call at the Air India offices to collect our tickets for next day. The place is empty, we are the first at the counter, it shouldn't take long. Mr Sen takes our passports and stares at them for some time, quite fascinated by what he finds in their empty pages. Then he starts to prod very slowly at his computer.

What appears on the screen puzzles him. He calls up the counter to Mr Dutta to come to his assistance, and this leads to a long chat in Bengali when words like "out first ball" and "what a damn disgrace" surface to indicate their drift away from our boring tickets to the Test Match in South Africa. When Mr Dutta leaves there is the question of Prince Charles and Princess Di to be thrashed out. Which of these persons do we presume to be at fault? When we say we don't know or care Mr Dutta is summoned back to listen to such heresy.

Finally we get our tickets, saying quite an emotional goodbye to our old friends Messrs Sen and Dutta, and head for the YWCA. There are several girls at supper who are working for Mother Theresa; Dutch and American, fresh faced and enthusiastic over their "really good day" among the dying. I wonder what it must feel like to be tended by white girls who don't speak a word of your language. Better than the pavements perhaps. Perhaps.

We have a clean room with beds of cast iron and pillows of reinforced concrete, and I sleep little. My mind is full of street children and stray dogs, and I have a sudden sinking of the spirits. I shouldn't have come back, I'll make myself ill again fretting over the impossibly unchangeable. I drink bottled water - the curry was very salty - and finally go off into weird dreams that the Clintons asked me to redecorate the White House. I was wallpapering in lumpy anguish when I woke.

At the airport there is a man with a cousin in Walsall who I also have to regret not to know, though its getting nearer home and I'm able to assure him that we might meet. It is a curious fact, the status acquired by having relations "at home" and the conviction often expressed that England is a good and happy place, full of rich people. I often deny this during my stay but am not believed, and indeed there's something patronizing in the denial. Relatively most English are better off than most Indians; how many old pensioners could take a plane in the opposite direction to mine? In India pensions are a privilege enjoyed by the few.

We fly up India, and then take a taxi up a steep rutted road into the hills; it branches to go to Darjeeling but we head for Kalimpong, a journey of three and a half hours through forests, with a pale green river winding below us. The trees are enormous, changing as we climb from tropical to firs and pines, with fountains of ferns pouring between them. The road is narrow and often unfenced, with steep drops from its crumbling edges. It is the only road to Kalimpong and full of buses and lorries which we always seem to pass on corners, our wheels inches from the edge.

There are monkeys sitting grooming one another on the verges, and occasionally running out to grab a plastic container thrown from a lorry. They have probably turned into a junk - food community with rotten teeth and heart problems. Large painted notices on the rocks do little to soothe; "Arrive in Peace and not in Pieces", "Life is Short don't make it any Shorter" and then on a very large boulder "The woods are lovely dark and deep, But I have promises to keep And miles to go before I sleep" which is surprising somehow. There are also great big demands in green paint for Free Gurkhaland, a subject that is causing some unease on these huge wooded hillsides.

*

Kalimpong appears at last on a ridge, and we drive through the bazaar and up two miles of narrow road to our destination; Dr Graham's Homes, where we will stay in the Guest House. It is one of many houses scattered over the hillside, framed in woods and great clumps of poinsettias and giant yellow daisies. The hostel has wooden floors and whitewashed walls and smells of spicy cooking. A Dr Sprigg and his wife are permanent guests and he meets us at the top of the stairs and offers us a sherry. He is an eminent scholar, his wife bedridden after a stroke. Their company is going to be one of the bonuses of our stay.

Dr Graham founded the Homes at the turn of the century, to deal with the problem of Anglo Indian children from the tea plantations and from Calcutta where they were often neglected or abandoned. One of my reasons for coming to Kalimpong was to examine the records for links with tea planters, about whom I hope to write a book. I knew it would be a sad and somewhat distasteful story, and it was, but whatever his original motives were Dr Graham did the most amazing, the most miraculous job in covering these vertical hillsides with dozens of houses, schools, a church, playing fields. Considering the one road, in his time merely a pony track, the feat of lugging all that building material up the four thousand feet from the plains was stunning. He mellowed and broadened his views too, and there are thousands and thousands of men and women today who are grateful for his Homes and the happy childhoods they provided.

Louise and I share a small room where the beds are only slightly less unyielding than at the YWCA, but I sleep well most nights, and wake to early morning tea brought by Mila the cook. Mila is small, elderly, smiling, an untouchable who would still not be able to prepare food for many Indians, but who gives us three meals a day with the smile always on his face. We get curries, stews, and macaroni cheese, and there is talk of banana fritters but they never actually materialize. We eat at a long table in a very large dining room; four of us at one end of the table. All the rooms are huge, the lounge which nobody uses is enormous, full of unsat in chairs and unplayed pianos and wet unread books about missionaries.

We have to go to the bank to change our traveller's cheques, which means walking for fifteen minutes up the tree lined road to a point where taxis may be found. I get used to the way these stop at intervals to pick up six or eight more passengers, and the habit they have of turning off the engine to save petrol. It is a fairly scary road, like all of them, but also seductive, with vast panoramas of Himalayan foothills and wooden houses perched on the edge, framed in scarlet and yellow flowers, and lolled on by Nepalese women and children, all ravishing.

Kalimpong was recently partly burnt down, but there is still a lot of it left, the small shops open to the road, their owners sitting on stools amid sacks of rice, bales of cloth, balloons, bracelets, and oranges. In one shop entrance a goat has its head down into a sack; there are plenty of goats, who look quite well, and a few dogs who don't. Taxis, scooters, buses, jeeps stir up dust and between them moves a stream of people, because there are no pavements. I want to stop and photograph them all, in their gorgeous colours with their shiny gold-brown faces. Situated as it is, the meeting point of Nepal, Sikkim, Bhutan and Tibet, Kalimpong is host to some of the world's handsomest races. I try not to stare at them, and none of them stare at me, which is nice. They don't see a lot of tourists, but have a natural courtesy, and I only once meet a beggar.

We climb up a flight of battered stone steps to the bank, a dark cavernous room with a lot of people drifting round tables piled high with documents. Behind one of them sits the man who takes our travellers cheques and passports, and I prepare for a longish session with intervals to check up on the Test Match, but in fact he is prompt and efficient and with a flashing smile hands us a brass token to take to the cashier at the counter. There is a queue, but we are dealt with straight away, and this I find a bit embarrassing. Is it colour, age or tourist status that gives us preference? I mumble apologies to the waiting line, but they don't seem to have noticed.

With our wads of rupees we visit the Arts and Crafts centre, placed on a plateau with spectacular views, but a ramshackle affair dumped down in the dust with no effort to make a garden round it. We buy bags for practically nothing, and I soon find that everything here costs practically nothing; taxis, oranges, bracelets, clothes, all so cheap. Apart from the bags there are only some Tibetan paintings, gaudy and modern, and we dream of what we could do if we could run this place.

Dreams only, foreigners can't buy property here or even settle, without relinquishing their passports and their British nationality. I feel a slight jolt at the news; the two hundred years in which my family has been in India suddenly of no account; the thirty years in which I was a much-better-than-them Memsahib absolutely forgotten. How strange, but then how right and how relaxing. India and I are equal now, or rather I am on sufferance and must know my place. To celebrate this emancipation, we eat in a cafe, curry puffs and coffee, delicious but something I wouldn't have done in the old days. Those awful Old Days which I feel falling away from me at last.

Thursday. Today we visit one of the monasteries, a long taxi drive up the hill, passing the army headquarters here, all white painted stones and fat labradors being exercised by orderlies. The monastery is in a spectacular position and picturesque in a way, with its flags fluttering and boy monks sitting round the entrance in purple robes. We walk round the outside, turning the prayer wheels, as does the taxi driver although he is a Hindu. Inside a lot of little candles don't expel a peculiarly unpleasant atmosphere, the dark and sinister side of Tibetan Buddhism, whose symbols of demons and restless ghosts adorn the walls. It's a disappointment; I'd expected peace and light within and flowers outside, instead of an untidy parking yard with not a blade of green to be seen.

I'd imagined myself spending early morning meditation sessions in a monastery here, but am thankful to get out of this one. There are several more, but I don't want to see them. "My" kind of Buddhism is different, more Western, cleaner and tidier; the scraped gravel gardens of Japan's Zen monasteries would be more appealing. A taxi arrives and a very old monk climbs out, carrying the shopping, tottering along with no help from the lounging boys. These value judgments, made from ignorance and prejudice, are un-Buddhist. Whoever is enlightened around here, it certainly isn't me.

Friday. I walk up the tree shadowed road to the office, where are stored the archives I want to examine. I get to know this road well; the walls with tiny white potentilla climbing up them, a tree that spreads branches bearing a thousand giant daisies, firs that droop and others that spring upwards, stone steps lined with yellow un-named flowers, bamboos, palms, a glossy leaved shrub with white or pink flowers that smell like jasmine, and everywhere the flaming riot of poinsettias. I pass women in saris and embroidered skirts, and men bent double under loads, with straps across their foreheads like mules. Scooters shoot round corners with girls in floating drapery on the back.

Filled with Mila's omelettes in the morning, or his curries after lunch, the road becomes familiar and loved; so dry with dead leaves crunching underfoot, so twisting and shifting under its shadows, so cornered and exciting, never knowing who will appear, wearing what, carrying what mysterious bundle of leaves on their backs. I wish I could paint, blending the flowers and leaves and shawls, and through the tree trunks the great grey hills.

The office is dark and cool, and I work at a table under a light. The records are kept in big volumes dating back to 1917, each page devoted to one child; his or her name, birth date, arrival at the Homes, parents names and nationality, and a brief account of the background. Tea planters feature largely in the early volumes, and I recognize some of the names as they approach the war. After that, there are only a few predictably. They give paltry sums for their children, sometimes a lump amount with instructions that they are to be bothered no further. Many of the children are rescued from Calcutta, from backgrounds in the railways or later the army. It is a depressing tale of desertion, drunkenness or death. In every case the children are given English names, George, Dorothy, Grace, never called after their mothers. I'm quite glad to step out into the sunshine and walk back through the poinsettias to lunch or tea.

Sunday. On a misty Sunday morning nothing seems more peaceful; Thomas the cat fed with egg dozing on the doorstep; clouds hiding Kanchenjunga which on clear days floats high above lesser foothills like a fairy palace. We go down the town after lunch and Louise buys Tibetan boots, beautiful but not really strong enough to walk about in. I produce a few Urdu phrases for the ancient crone at the door who looks a hundred, but it turns out we are the same age. She points at her one tooth to prove her years, and I take out my top set and wave them about to prove mine, which reduces her to hysterics. She is creased and creviced like a walnut, and I wish, as I often do here, that I could talk to her about the life that has so worn her out. Many Tibetans fled at the time of the Chinese invasion and have lived off their skills since, making these embroidered boots, or jewellery or painted scrolls. The money they get from them here is pitiful.

We go onto a shop full of silver and turquoise jewellery, the work of Tibetans but sold by a smart, articulate man who makes much of us, giving us tea and aniseed and telling us of a forthcoming trip to Delhi to buy a computer. He weighs what we buy on little old scales, and then tots up the bill on a calculator; soon an Apple Mac will be in the corner of his dark and cluttered shop, though with the extremely erratic electricity supply of Kalimpong it may not be quite the asset he hopes. Apparently a lot of people latch themselves onto the mains with wiring of their own, thus getting a free supply but dimming the lights for everyone else.

We get a taxi to the Himalayan Hotel and twenty minutes after our arrival it returns with my coat which I left in the back seat. Since we argued over paying the small fare asked, this strikes me as a truly noble gesture, and I would have given the driver the coat if I had another. He drives away before I can even offer him a reward. There is an air of honesty about the place generally, we feel very safe here, and can wander down back streets without being jostled or threatened, much safer than I felt in Spain.

Monday. An eagle floats overhead, the hills have almost disappeared into a grey mist. We plan a visit to Darjeeling, and then on to Sikkim for a few days; Louise went there last year and says it is fabulous. We also want to go down and see the Dalai Lama, but both plans involve long drives down tortuous roads. Louise is quite unfazed by grinding along the edges of precipices for hours on end, but I wilt at the thought. I don't seem to want to do anything but sit sunning my knees and eating oranges and waiting for the snow palace to appear above the blue haze of the lesser mountains.

*

Tuesday. Darjeeling. I agree to come this far, but stalled at Sikkim, which I know I'll regret, but the description Dr Sprigg gave of the road really scared me; very narrow, very steep with such sharp bends that vehicles had to reverse to the edges of the precipices to get round them. Louise is disappointed but good natured about it, she is doing her best to adjust to my aged limbs and quailing spirits. I even found it nerve wracking coming here in a jeep with twelve other people and all the luggage, plus three more hanging onto the back before we'd gone very far. With four of us in the front, the man next to me had to have his knees each side of the gear handle, and as we ground up the one in two hillside there was always a nasty second when the driver mistook the gear for his trouser leg.

Everybody says Darjeeling is freezing cold, being a couple of thousand feet higher, so I'm wearing every warm bit of clothing I possess; and on top leg warmers and a waistcoat spun from my own sheep's wool three inches thick, coat, scarf and gloves. I can hardly move and what with the twelve of us and the fact that we have to go down to the river before we climb up again, am steaming gently with my legs stuck to the seat. In spite of this it is one of the most beautiful drives I've ever done, with the changing greenery and the views of hills and river. I see a tree fern for the first time and can't believe it. Trees rise straight without side branches so it's like driving through a cathedral. Tea gardens drop away as we approach Darjeeling, bringing back dreary memories. It must be difficult to pluck the bushes on these steep hills. Pluckers are paid twenty five rupees a day I'm told, lucky them, that's 40p. It's a pittance but a lot more than they got in our day.

I unglue myself from the seat and we collect our bags, which we're glad to find are still there since they were tied on by a bit of string out of the glove compartment. Taxi drivers surround us shouting the large sums they want for driving us the five minutes to a hotel. Darjeeling being a tourist centre there is a different feel, not at first very pleasant. However as I can't walk up the steep road we have to agree to pay three times as much as the three and a half hour trip cost us to get here, and book ourselves into the Belle View Hotel; an understatement since the view you get from its top storeys is of the whole Kanchenjunga range.

Our room overlooks a wide square flanked on one side by shops and on the other by seats and trees, which is a kaleidoscope of colour, wandered across by monks and schoolgirls and men with ponies and burden carriers and police and a myriad of others out for exercise or just something to do. I take off most of my layers of sheep's wool as it is warm and sunny, and we go in search of food. We walk down past a row of street traders to a smart clean cafe, with bow windows full of sunshine and backpackers with the *Tourists Guide to India* spread out in front of them. Outside float the Himalayas, closer and clearer here, unreal. We have large cheap pizzas and big glasses of cold fresh orange juice and doughnuts. One could live in this window, and I suspect some of the backpackers do.

Afterwards we wander the shops, more sophisticated than in Kalimpong with a bookshop that rivals Waterstones and takes plastic. We buy books for the children in the Homes, a couple of paper backs each, some cards, a hardback book of poetry written by an Indian woman I should have heard of; all terribly cheap of course.

We carry these across the square as it begins to grow dusky. The ponies are trotting round still, and women with brushes and kerosene tins shuffling about sweeping up dung and litter. We pass one of these crouched by her tin as we make our way to the Windamere Hotel for tea. What a way to spend your days, and for what paltry sum I expect, but the result is a shining clean area for the rest of us to enjoy.

The Windamere is perched on a hill up a steep flight of steps, and is as extraordinary as we have been told; like stepping into a Kensington guest house in 1930. There is a huge coal fire, and tea is brought to us on frilly tray cloths, cucumber sandwiches and all. An Indian lady sits at the piano playing English folksongs, so we sip our Earl Grey to the strains of "Lavenders Blue Dilly Dilly" and admire the rather early Christmas tinsel and the plastic holly that festoons the pictures of old colonial celebrities in topees. Afterwards we drink beer, and are supplied with nuts and crisps by a waiter in white gloves. There are a few other guests to whom the piano player is very polite since they are staying there.

It's wonderful to have a hot shower, and next morning breakfast tastes really good after a walk to look at the early light on the mountains. Happy children are playing with a dog and I snap them against the snows. Further on less happy children and their mothers sit by the roadside begging. A portly man with a packet of biscuits distributes these amongst them, a Marwari gaining merit no doubt. I think of them as I eat omelette, toast and oranges, but am pretty hungry myself with only cucumber sandwiches since yesterday's lunch. As we drink our coffee the man who brought our breakfast walks past carrying a dead mouse. Well a rat would have been worse.

As we pass the street stalls I ask if I can photograph an old Tibetan man in a trilby, and then buy a (terribly cheap) waistcoat off his daughter. She admires the watch I wear round my neck, so I give it to her. It's gold but quite difficult to see and I shan't miss it. She asks where we are staying and says she'll bring some tea and cakes for us at four, and she does; Tibetan tea in a thermos which we drink sitting on the ground outside the hotel, and buns and biscuits. The tea is quite horrible, and after half a cup I feel sick. She explains how tea, butter, salt and boiling water are all shaken up together to make this revolting mixture, and I say it's delicious and look round for somewhere to pour what's left in my cup, but she is watching me closely to share my enjoyment.

She is a pretty woman, twenty six she tells me in good English. Her parents fled from Tibet in the sixties, but she was born and educated in Darjeeling. She has taken a teachers training, but it is very difficult for women to get jobs, which is why she has to sit by the roadside selling clothes. These are supplied by a Marwari who pays her Rs. 600 a month (ten pounds) on which she, her two brothers and a sister and old parents have to live. They have a house supplied by the council, and her brothers are still too young to earn. I take her photograph and address and she gives me a card on which she has written under the roses "To my dear Grandmother."

Next morning I'm woken with a cup of tea which I think has come from the hotel, but on sipping it I moan "Ugh, Tibetan tea" and leave it un-drunk. When I surface a few minutes later I'm embarrassed to find it is her again, arriving at the hotel at 6.30 a.m. with her thermos, and some silk scarves which she presents to us with a little bowing ceremony. I explain that I really like the tea, but not in the morning, and later we buy a bag of cakes from the cafe to try and make up for my rudeness. So she is there to help carry my bags down to the jeep and also a small sack of oranges which she presents to us; so Louise takes off a silver bracelet and gives it to her. Where this ritual exchange would have ended I don't know if we hadn't driven back to Kalimpong at that point, sensibly buying a spare seat this time so that the driver could reach the gear unhindered. He free wheeled for the first hour, only getting into gear for the last vertical drop to the river.

As we walk for the last time across the square, a crowd has gathered to watch a Gurkha band marching up and down playing their bagpipes. It is something to do with Free Gurkhaland, and they look extremely smart and handsome in their white spats with their tartan cloaks blowing behind them. Is this one of the good things the British did, teach them how to march and play Highland laments under the high Himalayas? Will they continue to do it when they are Free? It is strange to think that "Auld Lang Syne" will be echoing round these hills for years, and in the Windamere the strains of "Strawberry Fair" enlivening the teas of live in guests.

*

Christmas Eve. A tall cloud over Kanchenjunga, a white butterfly, a distant creaking bird, the scent of marigolds. Sitting in the dry mud I feel like writing a poem, the last two lines: "Home is a Hebridean rainbow and a cloud over Kanchenjunga. Is there anywhere that rainbow and that cloud Can meet?" Obviously not, and it's a pity I have to choose such eccentric landscapes to fulfil myself. Ants are bustling purposefully along dry stems and I envy them, knowing where they are going and why.

Hard to believe its Christmas tomorrow. Dr Sprigg set off in his blazer this morning, carrying bottles of wine for nuns and other friends. We shopped yesterday; a green sweater for Mila, Cinzano for the Spriggs, some toys for the children. Louise has brought crackers and we shall be going down to join them in the afternoon. Mila is going to roast a chicken and make bread sauce and we are to have three kinds of vegetable. And not a greasy dish or a soggy brussel sprout or an old Judy Garland film, how wonderful.

Boxing Day. Christmas day was wonderful. We walked up to church at 7.30, past the school and a splendid grove of sequoias, past a glistening frieze of snowy mountains, specially bright today, to a pew three rows from the front of this very large, English church. I wasn't wearing my Buddhist prayer beads but felt a little hypocritical not having been in a church for ages, and really only coming for the big communal breakfast afterwards. We sang carols and then sat for a long time listening to a sermon by a born-again Indian. He had Jesus in his heart, and we must too, but we must allow him to grow, not put him in a little box (he spread his hands to show how small) like they put the children of Calcutta.

At three we went down to the house where are staying the ten children who have no homes to go to in the holidays. Several of them rushed out to welcome us, clinging to our hands. I taught them "Grandmother's Steps" in the garden which they found wildly exciting, though the three year old twins never grasped the rules and refused to go back to base, standing on their heads instead. Afterwards we went in to the large room where the party was to be, around which were seated assorted Bursars, Padres, Caterers and their wives and friends, all silent and wooden. To Louise's slight embarrassment I got someone to the piano and organised Musical Bumps and Chairs, and then the Caterer's wife sprang up and organised several more games for which our little Darjeeling toys produced prizes. The children were wildly happy, the last game being Louise throwing a lot of chocolate bars amongst them to be dived for. All the onlookers were looking cheerful by this time except the Padre who was asleep in his chair.

Then we had tea, the children on a separate table, us standing around. I talked to the Bursar's wife; her husband a tall, elegant Sikh in a pale blue turban, she elegant also but looking tired and ill and complaining of how boring she found Kalimpong. I also reminisced with the Caterer about Naini Tal, the hill station I first went to when I was sixteen and where I met my husband Mac. It is his home and he went to the same school my brother attended for a short while. There are now good roads joining it to the other lakes where we used to go on pony treks along narrow mountain tracks. I don't think I would like it.

After tea the children get their one present each off the tree, cars for the boys, dolls for the girls, giving them more pleasure than the mounds of expensive electronics our children receive each Christmas. The Bursars etc. disperse, and we go outside to light a bonfire and sit round it singing; choruses such as "Jesus wants me for a sunbeam" and some Elvis Presley supplied by the teen age son of the house and his friends. This is the house of the youngest children, and has been in the care of the same housemother for fifteen years, with her blind husband who also plays the guitar rather well.

A small girl sits on one side of me, a ten-year-old boy on the other. She cuddles up, holding my hand, he lays his head on my shoulder. This desire for physical contact is of course the result of being taken so early from their mothers (this family has a particularly unfortunate background involving murder) and I find it both touching and sad. The housemother is an exceptional woman, warm and energetic and patient, but she gets children from birth sometimes and its impossible for her to give each one the touching and hugging he or she would get at home. Sitting under the glittering stars I wish I could stay forever, be a grandmother to these children, teach them the games and songs and stories I taught my own. The sadness I feel doesn't stop it from being the nicest Christmas I've had for years.

On the journey down from Kalimpong the taxi driver enlivens the journey by remarking at intervals "That is the very spot where five persons were killed when their jeep skidded". "There a bus overturned into the river drowning the entire occupants". He speaks good English, and tells me the oft repeated story; his education ended when his father died and he had to support the family. At the airport we have tea and toast, and to make conversation I ask him if he has ever flown to Calcutta. "For people like us that would be beyond our wildest imaginings" he says, and I feel ashamed at the silly question.

The Airport is crammed with people, and as usual it's impossible to hear what the announcements mean, but we eventually discover that our eleven o clock flight is to leave at 4 p.m. Luckily we meet a psychologist from South Africa and the time flies in conversation with him, including an analysis of our dreams. The one about decorating the White House he explains as being my white self returning to India, and redecorating my surroundings, clumsily but urgently. I'm impressed, it sounds convincing.

Calcutta is dark when we land, which makes the drive to the YWCA less harrowing. The bed is hard but I sleep soundly, and next morning set off to find the Old Park St Cemetery where among many other old inhabitants, my great grandparents are buried. "Symmetry" says the taxi driver, and nods confidently, and we drive for a long time through back streets, squalid beyond belief, and finally end up at a very new looking church. I lean out of the window and ask some passers by if they know the old cemetery. "Sahibs murgir" I say, laying myself along the back seat in a passable imitation of a dead empire builder, my hand beneath my cheek, my eyes closed. They shake their heads and click their tongues sympathetically thinking I'm referring to my own dead husband. It doesn't seem to surprise them that I should be sharing my grief with them, but they can't help. I tell the taxi driver to go back to the hostel, but on our way he suddenly grinds to a halt, and there it is.

It is a large walled area in the middle of streets, and at the gate I meet the man in charge, a very urbane and helpful person, who is apologetic that he can't help me find my ancestors as the man who has the map to the graves is away sick. It doesn't really matter, it is enchanting, these enormous mausoleums with their long, sad inscriptions stretch over a huge area and are now clean and well preserved, with flowering shrubs round them. I could spend all day in this ghostly record of heat,

44

disease, early death, pious acceptance. The atmosphere is peaceful, an old mali weeds with his dog snoozing beside him, its back against a tombstone.

The sadness of all those young lives lost is the other side of the coin of the reason why they were here at all, in the business of making themselves fortunes. It was a game of Russian roulette they played when they came to India, and these were the losers. My great grandmother, lying here somewhere, died leaving five children, but her husband retired with a large fortune and a great many jewels Unfortunately the wife he married when he got home turned into an alcoholic and he buried his diamonds in the grounds of his Cheltenham mansion, where her ghost is still reported to be trying to find them.

We drive to the airport along that terrible road, where patches of dirty water are being used to wash the rags that clothe the street dwellers. It's a pity that the last sight anyone gets of this city of joy is so desolating. The airport is on red alert as a result of a recent bomb attack in Assam, which means a lot of men with guns wanting to see our documents at frequent intervals. We trudge about for what seems hours, directed from one counter to another, and are eventually told to climb a flight of stairs. I protest that I can't, and am led to a lift. "We are anxious to assist aged and handicapped persons" I am assured. What with being mistaken for Mother Theresa and addressed as grandmother in Darjeeling, I feel a hundred.

We fly back via Karachi, spending the night at Doha in the grandest hotel I've ever been in. The contrast of this clean, sumptuous oil rich town with Calcutta is staggering. We drive to the hotel along palm lined streets, passing Pizza Houses and car showrooms, the cars that pass us all large and sleek, not a speck of dirt or a sad beggar in sight. We're quite tired after sitting in the airport waiting for three hours, with no refreshments, and the fact that it's nearly midnight the food laid out for us in the sumptuous surroundings of the Ramada is like the end of a fairy story. When we go up to our sixth story room there is a bath, the first we've seen for a month, with expensive soaps and oils at our disposal. I blot Calcutta from my mind for the space of time it takes to wallow in all this luxury, and sleep soundly in the first comfortable bed for a month too. If they found oil in Bengal would that too be transformed? A lot of Indians work here in the Arab emirates; the smooth and handsome head steward at breakfast is a Nepali from Kathmandu. It is a pot of honey they dip into, but they all want to go home as soon as they can afford it.

Six hours later we are flying over the snowy fields and roads of Kent and Sussex. It should be good to be coming home, but it doesn't feel it. Perhaps because the India I discovered on this trip felt more like home than the one I lived in all those years. Tomorrow is Edinburgh and opening the door of my house onto beige envelopes and possible burst pipes. All holidays end like this and I try, not very successfully, to feel lucky that I've had one at all. I feel changed, enriched, confused, unsettled. I swear if anyone starts whinging about their washing machine I'll kill them, after Calcutta. After Calcutta nothing will ever seem insufficient again. But I'll remember the road to Kalimpong too, and Kanchenjunga through the silver barked trees, and the endless procession of beautiful people I watched and talked to, and the children's hands in mine beside a Christmas bonfire. That above all.

JUXON
MY GREAT GRAND-FATHER

Juxon in Eastbourne

Although my family's links with India go back to the middle of the eighteenth century along another line, the story of the Jones family's connections with India start in 1840. My mother's story began with her great grandfather John Jones, Barrister at Law with a thriving practice in Exeter and father of eleven children: the youngest to reach adulthood was Juxon. At some unspecified date John Jones was ruined when a man for whom he had stood surety, a cousin called Stowey, failed and brought him down with him. The shock killed her great grandfather, and his widow Harriet had to take her family off to Ottery St Mary and live in a modest thatched cottage, the family house, Franklyn House in Exeter being left untenanted.

Juxon was sent to Christ's Hospital where he was as miserable as many others, notably Coleridge and Lamb, and at the end of that the son of the failed cousin produced enough money to put him through a medical training and loaned him £420 when he set off for India as a Surgeon to the East India Company. Stowey's debt was the source of much worry and remorse in the letters he wrote to his mother over the next ten years. My mother handed me this little pile of pale blue envelopes, Juxon's letters to his Dearest Mother with the comment that nobody else had been able to decipher them. They are wonderful.

When Juxon boarded the "Sophia" at Falmouth on a stormy day in February 1840 he was twenty five and optimistic; also relieved as he had spent six months waiting about for the right ship and the right conditions. His medical training over, Stowey's loan in his pocket, he was heading for a country where fortunes were quickly made even by junior doctors. His mother and his three sisters Netta, Sibella and Irene would have been equally hopeful. Even his brothers George and Tom might have expected the Pagoda Tree to drop something on their heads.

Even when ship board life had become a lot more comfortable for us who followed him, some things about it never changed. We walked up gangways into the same sharp scented, creaking, erotic unreal spaces. Sailing to India over 160 years ago you started, said Juxon, with "regular fisticuffs" over cabins, paid for but unallocated. He was pleased with his own arrangements. "Our raised floor is covered by a fine piece of oil cloth, I have put up two beautiful shelves, and newly arranged all my boxes and tables" he wrote while still in harbour, settling down for four and a half months. It didn't turn out quite the haven of peace he had hoped for though, for once at sea he was disturbed at all hours by "idle noisy cadets" drifting in and out.

There wasn't much romance either. The only female passenger, a Mrs Haines, sang like a nightingale and was "very chatty" but for little Juxon, weighing eight and a half stone, it was hard to reach her side to enjoy her chat. To begin with all thoughts of romance were dispelled by gales, reaching a crisis when they reached the Cape where the sea reminded him of "the hills and valleys between your house and Sidmouth", he told his mother. However, he still managed to enjoy a very good table till the last fortnight: "the best of wines every day and an unremitting supply of champagne twice a week". This helped everyone find the weather funny: "tumbling about afforded great amusement - very often dishes and plates and bottles would be swept off the table and all the passengers and their chairs would follow them to the other side of the caddy".

Horseplay and amateur dramatics and the nightingale tones of Mrs Haines whiled away the long days and weeks. "In the hot weather we had capital fun bathing at night about 20 fellows in, bathing, hauling up buckets of water and throwing them at each other". It was fun shooting albatrosses too, which were tame and defenceless. A surprising admission to his highly moral mother was that his cabin was called Crockfords because of the regular card parties held in it.

At last, at the end of June, Madras was reached, and the relief at being on solid land again was at first great. However Juxon soon found himself in a sort of hostel, provided by the East India Company for junior employees with nowhere else to go: "it is something dismal as the only furniture is a bad bedstead and much fallen mattress". I remember well those fallen mattresses of Indian Dak Bungalows, not only lumpy but alive with bed bugs. Juxon thought back wistfully to the noisy cadets and the cabin called Crockfords, and the performances of "The Rivals" and "High Life Below Stairs" on a stage composed of canvas with a Union Jack as a backcloth. "As I did not expect to find unfurnished rooms I brought no table linen or bedding except one pair of sheets", he grumbled to his mother who, nevertheless, must have been delighted to get this first news of him for four months.

Loneliness increased as "our old companions drop off every day, being appointed to their regiments, and all who had letters of introduction have capital berths horses etc. at their friends". Saddled with Stowey's debt and without contacts, his first impressions penned to his anxious women-folk were unenthusiastic: "We are surrounded by such a number of rogues, cheats and thieves that you would fancy that this were the Prison of Fleet".

He and his one remaining friend were easy prey as they wandered "all over Madras all through the Black Town, it is a most curious place...one evening I walked all through it with Dennys and you would have laughed to see us followed by a hundred people, all jabbering away at us like so many sprites, none going before us but three or four walking in the same line ordering all the people out of the way, declaring when we told them to be off that they were our servants".

As I read this first letter, I could smell the bitter burnt odour of frying gram rising from dust, and open drains; see the brilliant coloured cloth against the sugar pinks and shrieking yellows of the buildings; hear the hubbub of laughing voices offering to show this, help with that, guide, carry, clean shoes, find rooms, change coins, drive to any destination. For me the whole noisy explosion of light and smell was backed by bicycle bells and car horns. For Juxon there was the constant clatter of the hoofs of the ponies "pulling gigs or cabs called buggies which are of a vastly superior kind to London cabs".

Homesick in his empty room, he was quite cheered by the rumour that he, with many others, was to go to China where the Opium Wars were in progress. He would like to see the Chinese, "though I suppose we should seldom see them. From what I hear it is likely to be a distressing war as the Chinese will retreat before, burn and destroy everything that can afford us shelter...tanks will be poisoned I suppose as is not infrequent in these parts of the world".

Juxon always accepted the need for armies, and was beguiled to begin with by the bugles and flags of military stations, but he never liked war. Occupying forces were his reason for being in India, and at this period they were very occupied indeed in conquest and annexation, but he always preferred to stay behind with his pipe and use his rifle for shooting game. The East India Company, whose employee he was, needed a military arm both to extend its trading boundaries, and guard its frontiers and this he accepted without questioning the ethics of the situation. He always hoped, though, to become a civil surgeon, looking after the families of district officers. It was quieter and much better paid.

He managed to miss this "distressing war" and found himself instead in the big military depot of Dum Dum, eight miles outside Calcutta. He was dazzled. "Dum Dum is the principal artillery station in Bengal...it is a very pleasant and pretty place. Our mess house is the finest in India, it surpasses in magnificence most of the London club houses, having in addition to the mess room a ball room, billiard room, fine library and model room with guns and all such-like war-like instruments".

Even better, there was hardly any work. "I have only to see the patients once a day and have none of the dirty work. I have only to prescribe and as there are not 200 men at this station...I have very few patients at a time. I have but one hour and a half duty a day scarcely". Although he was designated Surgeon, in 1840 that didn't mean operating, at least in India. Hospitals were simply buildings in which to lay out the sick, who were nursed by male orderlies or low-caste women. Juxon's duties were to walk round morning and evening, prescribing medicines for diseases the causes of which were little understood.

This left a lot of time to fill in: "We breakfast and tiff (lunch) at each others houses and all dine at the mess at half past seven. We have a splendid band which plays every day in front of the mess house and Friday is always a public day for visitors...after dinner we always retire into the billiard room to play and smoke and drink our coffee".

Juxon found the ostentatious idleness of an officer's life in Bengal delightful. It was the kind of life his family had been bred for: "It seems so strange to be mixing in circles of gay splendidly dressed officers, with our band and splendid mess house, a thing which used to appear to me too grand for a little doctor ever to aspire to". Ottery St Mary had never been like this, and the women who read his letter round the hearth in their thatched cottage must have rejoiced with him. All

50

the scrimping and saving and borrowing had been worthwhile. Harriet's little youngest son was to be the success story that would set them all up again.

However, after three months he was writing: "We are now much more retired, owing to not having any vehicle of any kind we cannot get out". He and Dennys couldn't even afford to go to the mess, and it was with some relief that he heard he was to be transferred to a smaller station, Chinsura, and prepared there for a march to north India. Stowey's debt was already beginning to be a burden, and there was rarely a letter in the next nine years in which he failed to mention it.

For him and his fellow officers the nine hundred mile walk up India was quite a lark. They had horses to ride when they were tired, and servants to look after them, and tents to rest in at the end of each day. For the troops it was different. They bivouacked in makeshift hovels or in the open and walked the whole way on a diet of rice, tea and vegetable sauce. They ate cheap fly-blown fruit, a luxury unknown to them in England, and got dysentery; slept without mosquito nets and got malaria; and when they were near towns, frequented brothels and got venereal diseases. Even when they reached their destination (and many of them did not) they were not much better off.

Juxon's job on the march was to look after the sick and provide carts and palanquins for them when they were unable to walk. In fact there were only six stretcher cases and yet he complained of "all the duties - dispense medicine, keep accounts, journal and reports and so on". After only half a dozen letters it was established for me that this great grandfather of mine was extremely idle. Anything that looked like work always appeared to him as some sort of affront or imposition.

Medicine was obviously not his real interest, it probably never had been. Sons of ruined widows went in whatever direction seemed most profitable for the family as a whole. His own preference would have been to ramble about with a gun and return to a pipe and an hour with his fiddle, and better satisfied in a Devon rectory. But there was his Dearest Mother and his bevy of sisters depending on him to maintain the Jones tradition of gentility. They sat like queen bees waiting for the four worker sons to sustain them.

As they got further north, the weather improved, and for the last three weeks of the march "the weather was deliciously cool and fair all the time and our marches in the morning had all the charm of a walk in an English fine summer's day". Three and a half months after leaving Chinsura he arrived in Meerut "in as good spirits and health as a mortal could wish to be". He had only lost one of the five hundred men in his care, more from luck than good management. In the hot weather troops dropped dead in hundreds from heat exhaustion, and often had to fight a battle at the end of these tremendous tramps across India.

Juxon and Maria among other Europeans in front of a fort, said to be Phillaur, at the time of the Mutiny.

Meerut, the biggest military station in India, was in a state of "great uneasiness". with its seven regiments being prepared for what was to be the abortive Afghan War. Juxon was attached to His Majesty's 8th Regiment, and soon in the throes of his first hot weather. By July he was "sick at heart from longing so anxiously for the rains, and every mosquito bite drives me mad, the scratching more mad, and the burring of any insect into a raving distracted fury. I occupy myself by going from one kind of chair to another and to the sofa and back again to a chair, then try two chairs, an infinite variety of maneuvers until quite exhausted I fall into a sound slumber for the quarter part of what remains of the day".

By my time there were hill stations to which most women retired during the hot weather, and senior men too, but in 1841 these were for the sick and influential only. Governors built themselves lodges in the pine trees of Simla and Mussoorie, and there were convalescent homes for the sickest and luckiest, but most people stayed down and passed the time as best they could.

"I have daily practice at archery, and throwing darts as I used at Taunton, besides amusing myself with making targets etc. keeping tame partridges and making habitations for them, training dogs, chiefly for tricks, attending to my horses etc.". The rains had cooled things down, and Juxon sounded quite jaunty, blessedly unaware that this was to be the first of nine such summers.

Towards the end of the rains he was posted to Kurnool, a smaller station, as doctor to the Light Dragoons, a lucky move that saved him from going with the 8th to Kabul, there to be annihilated along with the rest of them, bringing the Jones story to an end before it had begun. His journey from Meerut was the first of many similar epics: "26 hours packed in a small parcel without any provisions beyond brandy and water and some sandwiches...The roads were nearly every inch under water and I went over ploughed fields, hedges, ditches, through drains and rivers at a splendid pace of 2 miles an hour". Juxon's journeys, before the days of railways, would make a volume on their own.

By November, Juxon was happily reporting from his new quarters: "I have literally nothing to do, my duty is to attend the drill every other morning which will soon grow exceedingly tiresome though at present rather agreeable". Boring old drill was better than another possibility, being posted to a native regiment, for as he confided to his womenfolk: "being with a native corps is worse than useless to a professional man. I think it would be more satisfactory to treat dogs and horses than natives"; a remark that undermines the oft-repeated statement that it was the memsahibs who took racial prejudice to India.

There was another worry about Indian troops. In the mid nineteenth century they were not altogether trusted, there was an uneasiness as to how they would react, particularly when asked to fire at men on whose side they might prefer to be. There are a lot of references in Juxon's letters to "shameful" events, when men turned and ran or, even worse, joined the enemy. Eventually the Indian Army gained a reputation for loyalty and dependability second to none, which is why it came as such a shock when some of them joined the Japanese in the Second World War.

Juxon, not given to introspection, neither questioned nor examined his views. What occupied him was the alarming news coming down from the Afghan passes of the first major defeat of a British army. India watched this Afghan War with interest, Burma too, but Juxon took himself off to a hill station, and was able to forget the humiliating tidings from Kabul for a while "luxuriating in an English climate English manners and customs, frost and snow and fireside, a perfect picture of home, there is nothing Indian about us except the shivering blacks". They could shiver away for all he was concerned, he was not there to minister to their ailing bodies and never, sad to relate, showed sympathy towards them.

He was moved, in these magical mountains, to try to describe his wonder: "I can see from my verandah the infant Ganges and the juvenile Jumna taking their silvery ways as far as the eye can reach nearly, and then disappearing for a short space of time and showing themselves on the other side of the hills in the boundless plains where their course is indicated by bright glittering spots appearing at intervals all the way to the horizon on either side east and west". One day was specially marvelous: "over our heads was a black canopy, a perfect dome of dense clouds, beneath the margin of which the whole view of the plains, hills, valley, rivers, towns, cities and countries appeared with a clearness and brilliancy which I can compare only to a glimpse of the heavenly regions".

From this delightful eyrie, where he only had to visit the hospital every other day and complained even about that, Juxon was sent as assistant civil surgeon to the beautiful valley of the Dun river. Civilian posts were still, at this time, in the gift of John Company and Juxon was much encouraged. Civilian doctors were better paid and could take private patients. Stowey's debt weighed a lot less at the prospect of this posting becoming permanent.

It was just like Devon in Dehra Dun, all rolling green hills and sparkling streams, and there were no troops to be attended to even fitfully, so that he could enjoy his "sweet pretty little house and garden" and magnificent shooting. He even took up sketching, breaking off the "very agreeable task of attending ladies, the chit chat with them so much better than talking with none but whiskered dragoons."

Into this little idyll was brought the news of the final disaster in Afghanistan, which had a shattering impact all over India: "Never was the country in such a state, perhaps the worst thing is that no one puts the least confidence in our rulers...we all suppose Lord Auckland to be a raving distracted man...it seems strange indeed to me to be in a country where all feel as if they were sitting over a mine with a fearful chance of its exploding. The papers teem with dark forebodings - which certainly terrify the timid heart. The country is almost without troops throughout the greater part, and in case of an outbreak...there is no power to suppress it and the whole country seems threatening it in every direction - there have already been three instances of troops marching many miles to overawe rebellions".

How the gentle hearts at home must have thudded to this news of the first Afghan War, but in spite of the minefield in which they were all living Juxon was able to assure his mother and sisters that in Dehra Dun there was "the most constant whirl of gaieties I ever witnessed, we scarcely once a fortnight dine quietly at home, balls, theatricals, picnics, dinners and visits take up all our time".

Dost Mahommed, the deposed ruler of Afghanistan, was sent to Dehra Dun: "Dost Mahommed with a great party of Europeans are in camp 200 yards from my door, red coats, swords, bugles etc. throng in every place, the very fields and valleys are filled with strolling jacketless soldiers, the game is all driven away..." Bad for the shikar it may have been but what heaven for the troops, away from heat and dust in their easy role of guarding a helpless Amir.

Juxon's main preoccupation was to get himself permanently posted in the Dun valley, but it all fell through, because on August 14th he was writing from Delhi: "It is an abominable detestable place, hotter than I have hitherto visited, dusty and dirty...Delhi is the great magazine of the Upper Provinces and I have the care of the Europeans and natives employed there". The pride of the Mughal Empire, the city of palaces and gardens, was now an enormous arms depot.

Juxon played a little cricket and made himself a bath, bemoaning the fact that "the gentlemen are eight or ten times more plentiful than the ladies...so I am afraid of some signal disgrace". Vaguely he wished he could get himself posted to some fighting frontier, there to earn medals to stick on his small chest. Medals, like some sort of mating plumage, were his only hope of attracting one of the few available ladies.

When it got cooler things improved. The Afghans had been temporarily quietened and the new Governor General, Lord Ellenborough, was celebrating in style, there was "an eternal hurly burly of parties, dinners, reviews, durbars cricket matches and what nots". At one of these entertainments Juxon met Dr Brydon, the only survivor of the retreat from Kabul, but doesn't record their conversation. The poor doctor had probably told the story so many times that he fled from anyone who approached him with an eager look and the words "I say how does it feel to be..." on his lips.

It was a year later that Juxon got his first and last experience of war at close quarters. The war in question was in Sind, a bleak desert country, the taking of which was strategically important but of course morally indefensible. Juxon was chiefly bothered about the prospect of being servantless when called up: "I must wash my own linen and feed upon biscuits", he told his horrified women folk, "there will be no well within a mile of the place you halt at, you can't buy provisions for yourself, you cannot possibly wash or cook for yourself". If you were a Jones you couldn't do that even in Leamington Spa, where Harriet and her daughters had moved.

However at first it wasn't too bad: "I am out with a regiment of cavalry for the purpose of dispersing the Baluchis who are collecting for their annual excursion about the country for plunder...we have lots of races between our people and the horsemen of the country. They are such picturesque figures, their horses little fleet animals that beat most of our large horses".

The one thousand strong cavalry brought in by the British created a lot of problems in a country so dry and fodderless, and it was no surprise that "the grass cutters went out and were set on by Baluchis who annihilated 100 men". In fact the novelty soon wore off, and Juxon forgot about medals, discovering that "war is certainly a disgusting, barbarous business, the life one leads during a campaign is no better than that of a brute, no rational employment, beer drinking and cutting throats are scarcely the only purpose for which we were born, yet they are the only things done during our wars. I don't care who knows it, I would rather be a civilian than the greatest hero".

Juxon's feelings were not typical. I have read a good many accounts written by young men who went to India at the same time, and they couldn't wait to get into the action. Whenever they heard of a "row" or "skirmish", they declared how "capital" it would be to be there. Partly it was boredom, but it was also a lot to do with loot, which was systematically (and sometimes haphazardly) divided amongst the winners. The "treasure" collected after the sack of large Indian cities was immense, and for the troops was the single biggest incentive to enlisting.

In England at this time, poverty and unemployment were alleviated by the great railway boom, which kept a lot of young men from the desperation of "taking the shilling". A young contemporary of Juxon scornfully stated that "we actually want men to be bribed to fight for their country's cause, a somewhat mongrel state to have arrived at". Your motherland might scorn and starve you, but you were still supposed to love her and fight for her to the death.

The oddest part of these wars that won the Empire was the way that aged and incompetent generals, leading badly paid and poorly housed troops, still managed to get the better of the other sides. Then there was wild license, a kind of running amok that seems more appropriate for Mongol hordes than disciplined European armies, if such these brutalized men could be called. The perks of victory in India were very great, and though unfairly distributed, everyone got something.

The war in Sind was simply pillaging and small scuffles between the British and the Baluchi tribesmen who were harrying and plundering an exhausted country. It was not noble, or even exciting, and it was with enormous relief that into this dustbowl of heat and futile slaughter came news of Juxon's release. He had been posted to the small station of Hansi, forty miles from Delhi. In this backwater he was to spend the next five years; which doesn't say much for his skill as a surgeon during a time of great battles, producing many sick and wounded.

While he waited to leave, there were billiards and trios on the violin, between sorties. The great autumnal sickness, thought to be caused by exhalations from the stagnant drying rivers, produced much fever which decimated the army. In September he was called over to a neighbouring town to help, a tiresome chore: "I rode at least 8 miles in water up to the flaps of the saddle so my legs were in the water for more than three hours and my head exposed to the boiling sun, a most unenviable situation".

It wasn't as bad as his final march from Sind, when he himself had contracted the malaria from which the men were dying: "I was unable to ride and was therefore carried on the heads of coolies - these fellows shook me to pieces, in fact I suffered as if I had been at sea in a heavy gale, for I did little else but vomit the whole way from Sirsa to Hansir. The marches being very long, I never got to my halting place till one or two p.m. half grilled by the sun - after two of these trips I was obliged to take half the journey in the morning and half in the evening.. I could hardly sleep or move and the way I fed myself was by putting my face into a dish and sucking up its contents. In fact my life was at the last flicker - if I had another march to make I should never have reached my destination alive".

One more march and no marriage, no grandmother Annie, no me.

He was restored on arrival with mulled wine, eggs and tea every hour, and soon announced that he had bought a beautiful house for £80, which would be made more perfect when his mother's portrait hung on its wall: "Never lover so fondled, caressed and sighed and wept over the picture of his adored as I shall over the dear resemblance of you my mother", he rhapsodized, in language quite appropriate for a Victorian son.

By June, waiting for the monsoon, he was finding Hansi tedious and was even reminded of the worst period of his life, his school-days at Christ's Hospital. Other more famous pupils agreed with him. Coleridge remembered the headmaster's sinister dirge: "Boy, the school is your father, boy the school is your mother,..." and so on through brothers, sisters and cousins, impressing on his little victims their utter dependence on his regime of hunger, fear and prayer. Charles Lamb described being terrorized by the King's Boys, pupils being trained by William Wales, co-navigator with Captain Cook, for their tough life at sea. These deliberately hardened youths called themselves the First Order and the cry that they were coming sent shivers down every small spine. Tiny Juxon, so bullied in between being ordered to prayers "in an almost monastic closeness of succession" as Lamb put it, wrote in his thirtieth year: "If I had fifty sons I would not send them to that place even for food".

Hansi didn't produce such terrors, but was so hot and boring that he read anything he could lay his hands on, though he had to admit that "if the wind of the punkah chances as it often does to turn over half a dozen pages, I am seldom at the trouble of turning back to where I was reading, but go on at where the wind has opened the page". From the novels of Lady Burn, he turned in desperation to Hindi Grammars, not only out of boredom but because he needed to pass a language exam to get promotion.

Not far away things were moving towards the annexation of the Punjab in the Sikh Wars. Juxon's letters from sleepy little Hansi are full of descriptions of battles, of huge losses on both sides, of great guns being lugged hither and thither, and of every available man heading towards the Sutlej river, himself excepted: "The road is so thronged with poor officers trying to get on to Ferozpur that no one scarcely can procure bearers for their palkis. I heard that Dennys was seen some 40 miles from this, walking along the road without his palki and of course without half his necessary traps". The picture he paints has an amateurish air about it. What were all those officers doing away from their regiments in the first place?

It was a bloody war, but it had its funny moments: "The Kalsas (the Sikhs) in the fort found out that a certain bugle which sounded at sunset called the officers to dinner and they somehow found out where they dined and one fine evening some quarter of an hour after hearing the said bugle, they let off a gun... and the sequence was the presence of a 241b cannon ball in the mess room, not exactly in the room as it passed through both walls." The cannon ball missed the General but dinner was ruined.

Juxon was moved to Delhi for the cold weather, but had little to do, and found time to fall in love with a General's daughter in spite of "a cutaneous eruption" on her face. He didn't win her, and the following autumn was back in cosy Hansir contented with tea and coffee mornings, "quoit playing, shooting, gossip, mustard and cress and delicious bread and butter".

He was now thirty one, with Stowey's debt only slightly reduced, and with a new and agonising worry, a demand for £800 to pay the debt of a defaulting fellow officer for whom he had stood surety. It was his father's story all over again, and he suffered tortures all through the hot weather, not helped by a nagging toothache.

Apart from these worries, life made few demands: "All my friends meet at my house in the morning, after a cup of tea and a cheroot, we stroll down to the tank. Some fish, some stroll about, some take a steady constitutional till the sun gets hot and then come home to breakfast. All this of course after the performance of our morning duties, parade, hospital".

In September, he heard that the debt for which he had stood surety had been paid, and his relief was exquisite: "now dear mother I can write in great spirits - indeed I was just on the point of commencing my letter with a hip hip hooray, with many wa was and och ochs but that I feared you might think I had gone mad - not melancholy mad - can you guess the cause of this exuberance of spirits and folly? George Harriott has paid his debt to the Agra bank. You won't want me to write anything after that piece of good news. He sent me a letter which accompanied your last informing me that he had paid £800.... I need not attempt to describe the relief this news has been to me and will be enough if I tell you my dear friends have fully expected me to give a champagne supper to the station which you know is the common way in this country of exhibiting any joyful event and exceeding good fortune such as coming suddenly into £5,000 a year, the removal of some tough old senior captain, anything of that sort.... Now I am renewing my old plans of marrying, going home, or going home and marrying.... of saving money hand over hand. If you want any money now is the time to mention sums. How many thousands eh?".

At the same time, he had the pleasure of new neighbours, a young married couple called Hockin who came from his part of Devon. It was they, according to my mother's story, who led him to the clock in Exeter three years later, and to his first meeting with Maria.

In the spring, the Sikh Wars entered their second phase, but Juxon embarked on his eighth hot weather uncalled on, though ready to comment at length on army strategy, and the uselessness of generals, opinions he shared with Lord Dalhousie who noted with deep disgust "the spirit of croaking is characteristic of the army". Dalhousie was to wield a new broom as Governor General, but though much depressed by conditions in the British army, he was no believer in the rights of any oriental; the sooner Britain took over what was left of the Indian sub-continent the better; and Burma too for good measure.

The winter campaigning season had the roads crammed with officers again, trying to get back to their regiments. "Charles Reynolds who has not seen his regiment for years has to leave his appointment and join them at Multan...Mr Edlin and many more doctors ordered from Calcutta to the army at Ferozpur". But not Juxon, who spent November "in glorious ease, watching the growth of my peas and cabbages". He spent a lot of time on the garden, ordering the digging of a well and watercourse. He was also in charge of the Post Office so his house was full of people for four hours every morning, drinking brandy and smoking cheroots while the mail was being opened.

Great battles being fought by the banks of the Chenab didn't alter his life at all, and he showed no patriotic urge to take part in any of them. "I take my daily constitutional walk at sunrise, and superintend my ice work, return to breakfast, play the fiddle or at billiards, take my gun and walk over the dusty weary looking country, then smoke my cheroot on return, talk about affairs in general read the papers if a paper day. In a short time I go to dinner, and find great difficulty in keeping out of my bed till 8 o'clock". Later, when a young cavalry officer was regaling his wife with tales of Chillianwallah he may have felt some regret at having missed out on the Sikh Wars, but at the time he felt none.

The chaos at the front confounded him, and as usual he blamed the men at the top, on this occasion the Commander in Chief, Gough: "I heartily wish some ferocious Seik would capture him and keep him safe". In the middle of the confusion "the King of Nepal came down from the hills with a large army and artillery...troops were immediately sent for from Madras...happily His Majesty walked back to the hills on falling sick in the Terai". The King must have kicked himself afterwards, when, the Sikhs dealt with, his own country came under the imperial hammer.

At last, in March 1849 an efficient general arrived and the Sikhs were finally routed, their country annexed. After all the excitement, which had filled his letters for months, Juxon approached his ninth hot weather flatly. He complained of a lot of "running about" when his commanding officer's child became ill, which was uncharacteristically callous. The Campbells had lost three children and were demented with worry.

But Juxon was now pitched into a mood of real depression. After nine years without home leave he was physically and mentally stale, listless, demoralised. "I take, or rather for the past week have taken, no solid food. Morning and evening I take a long exhausting walk - while indoors I read Persian for 3 or 4 hours so that my mind may have exercise too. I hate the approach of night and of day alike, for at each period I am equally weary, weary, weary"; and this without, or perhaps because of, having very little to do.

By August he was feeling better and starting seriously to plan for his return home the following year. It was going to be a long haul: by palki to Delhi, then horse and carriage to Allahabad, and finally a two week steamer trip to Calcutta before the three month boat trip home.

On February 6th 1850 a letter triumphantly announcing "Hansir for the last time" was a bit premature, because it was March 20th before he finally got off. His application for leave had to catch up with the Commander-in-Chief, which it finally did in the Khyber Pass. The mind boggles at such unwinding and crisscrossing of red tape all over India; that the exalted thumb mark had to be put on pieces of paper as unimportant as Juxon's.

His long journey down to Calcutta, the last he would make as a bachelor, was tedious and expensive, and he had miscalculated his finances as usual. The first forty nine miles took sixteen days. "The seat of canework of my palankin was in such a dilapidated state that I found rest for the journey solely upon a very sharp cornered bar which fitted neatly between two of my vertebrae". He got rheumatism and a heavy cold, was bitten by two enormous monkeys, and arrived at a friend's house sore and exhausted.

There he recovered and thought he was better organised for the next stage, which was by horse and carriage "where I had my bed prepared and beer under my pillow". He had changed his mind about going by steamer and intended to drive all the way to Calcutta, not a good idea as it turned out. The horses provided were so poor that he had to get out and push or drag when things got difficult: " I commenced each day's journey as early as 4 o'clock in the hopes of getting to the end of our miserably short stage, reduced from 90 miles to 50 or 40 each night, but all in vain, for 10 o'clock with the blazing sun that made the carriage too hot to be touched, found me each day labouring till I was really exhausted. Sometimes after wasting hours in getting over little more than a mile of ground I was obliged to send to some distant village for coolies to draw the vehicle... I moved on at a snail's pace. Sometimes I found no horse, sometimes no harness, at the changing places...then a brute of a horse would kick all the harness to pieces and so on. I am sure I have fallen at least 2 stone in weight".

Worst of all, this discomfort had cost a lot, and Calcutta was very expensive, a pound a day for bed and board. His passage home cost £130 and his leave pay, which he had also miscalculated, was to be £90 instead of £150 a year. His mother and sisters, hoping for a Nabob, were getting the same man they had sent out, Stowey's debt finally repaid but that was all. The long and rapturously awaited reunion was perhaps a little spoilt by this. When he married later that year, he had to borrow again from Stowey and it was years before he was solvent.

Juxon's letters home during his first ten year spell often talk of his family, usually with affection coupled with anxiety because they were all finding life a struggle. His second brother, Frank, set up as a schoolmaster in Ilfracombe, but had more children than pupils, twelve before his wife died of exhaustion. Tom, the eldest and Bertram his third brother were sent to Newfoundland and there, after a drifting life, Tom died of tuberculosis. Bertram, who became a Dean was perhaps the one success.

The choices for the girls were the normal ones at the time: marriage, endless pregnancies, several child deaths, widowhood usually in "reduced" circumstances but sometimes blessedly well-provided for; or a single life centred on the church, never ceasing to be the daughter of the house, second rate, the presser of dead flowers and preserver of old letters and faded photographs.

MARIA MY GREAT-GRANDMOTHER

Maria in Eastbourne

After his return from India Juxon had fled Leamington Spa, ostensibly hounded out by heartburn. More likely it was his search for livelier company. His mother Harriet was a very holy lady. She wrote several letters to Cardinal Newman which he kindly answered, a correspondence that ended abruptly when he "went over" to Rome.

According to my mother he met Maria under the church clock in Exeter. Maria was introduced to him by the Hockins, friends in Hansir, to whom she was related. She was the youngest daughter of a Captain Thomas Stirling, born in Jamaica but retiring to Dartmouth to marry. The family who could look back, in a roundabout way, to the Earl of Glencairn, produced some lawyers and a friend of Pusey's who married his sister. In spite of these credentials there were four daughters to marry off. Maria was twenty when she met Juxon, who had been dreaming of a small docile wife but who looked up into her blue eyes (she was nine inches taller) and was smitten. They were married four months after their meeting.

No sooner married in January 1851 than Maria was pregnant, and the carefree leave Juxon had dreamt of in steamy Hansir was spent with an ailing wife, who, after a "turn" on Exeter station had to be wheeled round in a bath chair. Maria had ten children without trouble, but the fuss made of this first pregnancy was part of Victorian lore. There seemed nothing in the least ridiculous in pushing a twenty-year-old round in a bath chair, gentle, frail and delicate as upper class ladies had to be.

Maria recovered her strength sufficiently for them to visit the Great Exhibition in June, when it was extremely hot, and the "throng of common people" added to the discomfort Juxon wrote to his dearest but discarded mother and sisters in Leamington. Moreover their boarding house offered them beds full of bugs and they had to sit on the floor all night, which must have reminded him of the fallen mattresses of Madras.

A few of his letters survive and show him to have been besotted with his young wife, quite ill when forced to leave her for a few days. Then on September 20th she began to have pains in the night, which produced a "poor little dead girl" two hours later. Juxon tidied her up and they both went back to sleep, not particularly disturbed. He was now able to plan an earlier return to India, though it later transpired that he had run out of money as usual, and staunch cousin Stowey had to be touched for another loan, which took several years to pay off. They sailed on December 20th and stayed out in India for seventeen years. Their children stayed with them, partly because there was then no great stigma attached to such arrangements, partly I presume because there was nobody at home who could cope with eight of them, and the Holiday Homes of our day didn't exist.

For a year or two Juxon continued to write to his mother who managed to survive until 1867, the year before he retired. It was the same old tale of "pecuniary difficulties". In March 1852, just after their arrival, these were "most dreadful". "I owe every tradesman in the country, you cannot imagine how sorely afflicted I am with poverty and how unable I am to pay even the postage of a letter". From Ludhiana, where he was posted in April, the full extent of the mess was revealed to his mother. He had drawn six months pay in advance and when he got to Calcutta found that his funds had fallen into arrears to the sum of £701, and this in spite of Stowey.

By May he was busy selling everything: £8 for his watch, £5 for his fishing rod, £12 for knives and forks. Maria was expecting a baby in August and was kept in the dark as much as possible. She was of course "lying up" and they spent a lot of the time in her room eating mango fool; presumably they still had their spoons. Juxon only had two hours work a day, and in spite of the heat and his worries, was in love and happy.

Then suddenly, and almost on the day of her expected confinement, they were ordered to Bengal where he would embark for Burma where the second war was about to begin. For reasons not explained Maria could not be left behind, so off he humped her, in the heat and monsoon rain, on a journey almost Biblical, the child due to be born, the parents without plans or resources. Another epic journey began. "We were carried nearly the whole night on the top of the bearers heads, who slipped and tumbled at every step, terrifying the poor gentle, tender Minnie (his name for her) out of her wits and endangering her life too, for a fall would have killed her had she even escaped immersion in the water which was often up to the men's waists. We were set down in the fields for hours while our bearers left us in search of shelter from the rain which was pouring in through the roof in 2 places, without food or rest we at 5.a.m. continued our journey through the fiercely beating rain till eleven when we found shelter again. I was obliged to walk nearly all the way, often up to my middle in water."

At one of the staging or Dak bungalows they managed to find shelter and Maria went into her second labour and produced "a pretty little girl, dead of course." Two dead babies could have shattered Maria, but she seemed to get over it quickly, and on arrival in Calcutta they installed themselves in a house in the middle of a "pretty meadow", and started to socialise. Burma never materialised, but Maria was soon pregnant again. In the few letters of hers that survive she refers to "my event" as a sort of yearly date, like the Derby.

In October 1853 she produced her third daughter, this one alive though small. This was Minnie, whose pet name was Pins. Maria found she couldn't feed the baby and after trying bottles they resorted to a wet nurse. Juxon referred in a letter to "these unpleasant and unprofitable nuisances" who succoured his children. It must indeed have been hard for him and Maria to watch their babies suckle at the breasts of low caste women, the only ones who would accept the job. On one occasion they used an English girl, the fifteen year old wife of a Sergeant whose own baby had died.

The baby's arrival coincided with that of Maria's elder sister Henrietta, who was married within six months to a railway engineer, six feet three inches tall and on a salary of £1000 a year so quite a catch. Juxon, who had to pay for the wedding, was thankful when the next sister, Sibella, went to stay with Henrietta and her rich engineer. But all did not go well with Sibella. "You will be horrified to hear" he told his mother (why one wonders did he not spare these horrors) "that the last of the girls who came to India has left the home of her brother and sister and has joined herself to the lowest, humblest of the Railways people. She has been carrying on clandestine meetings with a needy adventurer - no European in the country could have been a more unsuitable match - and engaged herself to marry him. She ran away to the house where this man was a waiter - a mere servant (gasps from Leamington Spa) and then went to the nearest station to get married. However she repented of that kind promise and sent her lover about his business - and she has been received into the family of a half caste employee of the Opium Dept. and of course she is the associate of these people's friends".

It went without saying that "she is utterly lost, no one in this country can acknowledge her." She would have been better off with the white scars of leprosy, than the taint of consorting with Railway People. However the story had an unlikely ending, because in his last letter before leaving India Juxon planned to stay with the rich husband of this same Sibella in Calcutta. Her sister's prosperous engineer, on the other hand, had proved sickly and was long since dead.

Fourteen months after Minnie's birth arrived a son, Harry, and a year after that, in 1856, a tiny frail daughter Eleanor. By then the family were in Phillaur in the Punjab, and Juxon's debt had been reduced to £120 so that he was able to employ twenty servants and a European nurse. In December 1856 his flow of letters to his mother ended, but a few notes are preserved, written during the upheavals of the following year.

One of my mother's favourite stories was of Grandpapa and Grandmama in the Mutiny. She had them both: Maria in crinolines, with two small children and pregnant with a third: travelling down to Delhi with General Nicholson's army when the mutineers arrived. There for some reason they were separated, and wrote to one another from different parts of the Ridge, a handful of thin blue pieces of paper which she carried round with her for years. We all enjoyed this story, especially the crinolines, and it wasn't till after she died that I read the letters. When I did I realised that she had never in fact done so.

Neither of them went to Delhi (the dates were wrong) nor in fact saw much of the action. In the Punjab the Governor Sir Henry Lawrence was firm and capable, in contrast to all the other geriatric generals. He disbanded doubtful regiments and prevented the chaos and carnage raging round Cawnpore and Lucknow. There a lot of elderly out of practice military men were totally flummoxed by events they had never met before and never anticipated.

More books have been written about the Mutiny or the War of Liberation than of any other subject in the country.   Shock waves travelled round the world because Britain nearly lost the jewel in her crown, and without it the crown might have toppled off.   There had been other small revolts, harshly suppressed, but the general feeling was that Jack Sepoy would never be a traitor. Any country "ruled" by another would have causes of disaffection; slights, insensitive laws, ignorant and arrogant behaviour at all levels. One man was most responsible, Lord Dalhousie, Governor General from 1848-1856, whose appetite for annexation angered many of the large landholders. His final big take-over of the rich, powerful and beautiful kingdom of Oudh was the last straw.

But there were many other straws, and what set them alight was the order to bite the cartridges of the new Enfield rifles which were greased with pig and cow fat, both sacred animals to Muslims and Hindus. Sepoys started to refuse, to disobey, in military terms to mutiny. Then the hatred and resentment built up over time exploded in a rampage of murder, not only of officers but of their families. Jack Sepoy acted totally out of the character that the British had given him.

The British in the nineteenth century were disgusted by Hinduism, which they saw as all widow burning, infanticide and ritual strangling. They made strenuous efforts to break the caste of Hindu sepoys in order to Christianise them. Muslims were less suspect, but also pagans. It became a crusade, and to the sepoys a dreadful threat. To lose caste was a fate truly worse than death, because the effects of it stretched beyond the grave. The army in India at this time was divided between British troops on loan and paid for by the East India Company, and British officers commanding Indian regiments. In both the generals, according to the rules of promotion by seniority, were mostly old and incompetent.

The trouble started in Meerut. According to William Howard Russell, the Times correspondent, things could have been nipped in the bud, and the mutineers prevented from setting off for Delhi. He told of the "incapacity of an aged veteran general" who allowed the mutineers to march to Delhi from Meerut "with a regiment of English dragoons, a famous Battalion of infantry and field artillery within a few hundred yards" To give him his due, he had no bullocks (absolutely vital) and no medicines. Indecisively he then died, and two other generals went to Delhi, and stayed there for three months.

They waited for help from the Punjab and to bring it came John Nicholson "a man cast in giant mould with massive chest and powerful limbs" and also a reputation for winning battles. Here at last was an active and efficient leader, but it wasn't long before he too was dead, gallantly leading an assault. Two more generals dropped off before the battles were finally won, one of them Havelock was actually hit by a canon ball and not the victim of the ever present cholera. This and heat exhaustion killed far more of the British troops than actual battle

65

wounds, partly because of the ridiculous uniforms, long sleeved jackets and tight trousers and on their heads great heavy helmets to keep off sun and bullets. It was thought that sunstroke was the main enemy.

There were no pitched battles in the two years it took to quell the mutiny, but a series of skirmishes and one long siege in Lucknow. Here the little band of Europeans were thought to be starving because nobody had told them that the cellars of the Residency had been stacked with provisions. This kind of muddled lack of communication was typical, and if the rebels had been better organised, they would have prevailed.

The best description of the way the army moved and fought comes from Russell's despatches. He moved in from the Crimea to India and on the boat the news reached them at Alexandria. "Hurrah! Bravo! Lucknow is relieved" they all shouted. Perceptively Russell put his finger on the true horror of the situation, "that a subject race, black men, dared to shed the blood of their masters." Russell had no illusions about the British in India. "We are in India rather on sufferance and by force than by affection." he told his readers, many of whom would have been affronted by this unpalatable truth.

Russell moved up with the new Commander in Chief Colin Campbell, sixty five years old but physically and mentally alert. Russell described their progress: "The army had the appearance of some vast menagerie which ate up the land as it went like a plague of locusts" he said. There were twenty servants for each combatant; to fetch water, cut fodder, groom and feed horses, bullocks, elephants and camels and carry the commissariat for the officers. Crops were trampled and when fuel was needed the thatch from village houses was used. General Campbell's baggage alone stretched for eighteen miles.

Russell described their stops, when they camped. "The servants brought round tea for their masters, the syce brought round horses to the front." There was a mess tent where each officer had his servant behind his chair and breakfast was tea and coffee, with goats milk, bread, butter and chappattis, fish, mutton chops and curries. For dinner there was soup, fish, mutton stews, sweets, sherry, beer and sometimes champagne. All this was carried by coolies if not on the hoof or dragged by bullocks.

When Russell became ill he was carried in a "palki" where he had a shelf for wine, biscuits and preserved meat, books, a flask, powder, shot and a rifle. Into this leaned an officer. "Where is Ted Brown - the Chief wants up the heavy guns."? he told the Times Correspondent. In such a casual way was the battle commanded. Vital messages were sent by semaphore and luckily there was a copy of Pears Encyclopaedia at hand to learn it. Bizarre and slightly comical all this, but for the troops who were "tortured by flies, smothered in an atmosphere of dust, prostrated with heat and loss of blood from leech bites" it was different. It was truly a "devil's wind" that blew about their heads. At the end of the fighting the count was 2,054 killed in battle, 8,987 dead of heat exhaustion. It was no surprise that when a town was captured, men went mad with blood lust, enemy sepoys burnt alive "their skin crackling and their flesh roasting literally in its own fat" Russell said. Rape and pillage on a horrific scale were looked on as the natural rewards of Indian warfare.

After it was all over the Governor General read out a proclamation from various platforms, saying that Queen Victoria would now take over the country and things would be better. Not many Indians listened and those who did were sullen and disbelieving, with some justification. Attitudes inevitably hardened, Indians were no longer trusted, a deeper divide opened between them and their rulers who became more haughty and suspicious. Juxon and Maria reflected this feeling, even though they themselves had suffered little.

The arrival of mutineers in 1857 came as a complete surprise to them in Phillaur. Maria and the children with another family were sent across the river to Ludhiana, guarded by Sikhs who were hopefully loyal, and presumably housed with villagers. Juxon sent her notes, the first on June 6th. "Dear wife, we are all safe and sound here. I wish you were here but I trust you feel as safe where you are as we do. At first I was thankful that you were all gone, for we were taken quite by surprise - I was on the parade when the cavalry appeared by the butts. They could have caught us in a moment. The Seikhs with you are staunch I trust. If the bridge is broken the mutineers cannot escape, for troops are following them from Jullunder. I have been watching these fellows with a telescope and they appear to be pitching their tents. Mr Dobbin has just run a large gun to give them a shot. We are expecting the two regiments of infantry but they have not yet arrived. Our men did not turn out to fight but they did not encourage the mutineers to do any mischief. I must say goodbye and bless and comfort you and our dear little treasures. Henry." He was now using his second name, but it is easier to stick with Juxon.

Four days later Juxon wrote twice. 10 a.m 10th June. "Your letter of six o clock this morning has just reached me darling, I need not speak of anything but of my deep thankfulness for your safety my only treasure. The Force had nearly reached the river by this time, and then I trust that your terrors may be over. You will of course come over here, the men in the Fort will most likely run away when they see our force. All will be safe and quiet again by the time you get this. I need not say how bewildered with agony for your sake I have been since yesterday. I must not stop to add another word, God bless and comfort you and our little treasures."

It seems from this that the mutineers had got into the fort, or part of it. Later that day Juxon wrote another letter, a proper one in an envelope. "The worst is over dear wife, and I trust you will not suffer in health from the fearful terrors that have surrounded you for 2 days and nights. I was unable to sit down one moment and write to you darling yesterday, but now can do so. The sense of relief of the flight from Loodeanah is so great that I feel all cause of alarm has gone with those villains. I am looking forward to a letter from you every moment. The last news we had from across the water was that Olpherts wrote at half past four yesterday - viz that the occupants of the Fort had fled and he was going in pursuit of them. I hope dearest that you will soon come over here, for though the accommodation for you and the dear little children must be wretched, I think you would prefer our being together. Poor dear darling Minnie, I shall find you much altered, looking very wretched and pale and worn out? I hope not. How I should rejoice to see your dear face again, and those of our dear little treasures. Poor little Minnie, give her a kiss and Harry too and say Papa sent this kiss and this letter. My heart has ached for you poor Minnie and for poor dear Mrs Cox. I have felt one little consolation this moment in finding that in every station in India nearly there is fear and alarm. I allude to what Mr Stapleton mentions in letters from Rawal Pindi. Since writing the last words I have had a letter from Mr Griffiths. I hear this instant you are on your way here, I hope so dearest for I long much to see you all again. God bless you my poor suffering wife. I am deeply deeply thankful for the safety of everyone. Your loving husband."

Mr Griffiths seems to have been over optimistic, because next day Juxon's note was accompanied by boxes of silver and linen, lamps, gun cases and photographic equipment. "6p.m. 11th June. Dear wife, I have found a messenger just starting from the Fort for Loodeanah so I will send a few words with him. The coachman, syce and granoker (sic) will start from this at dawn tomorrow taking heaps of linen for you all. I sent keys of your two boxes and the drawers. It is to be left to the authorities to determine whether you can come. Nothing but your danger should induce you to come. Mr Dobbin is going tomorrow to Loodeanah, I have everything in the Fort except the contents of the Godown. I sent this open so I could send you a kiss for the children and tell them to give you a dozen of them. What fearful scenes you have gone through my poor pet. Henry."

There followed a list, not altogether legible, with "Dearest wife I send you nearly all the traps" at the top:
"1 chest of drawers in 3 durrees
Your three boxes
Gun case
Knife tray with...
I have kept 5 knives and 5 spoons, 10 things in all
I have sent the photographic box
The 3 lamps in one...except some parts"
There are a few other undecipherable items. It seems curious that coachmen, syces and Mr Dobbin could all cross the river, but not Juxon. Cutlery and sheets seem the last things anyone would have been worried about at such a time, but for Maria it would have been a comfort to feel soft linen beneath her cheeks. Servants staggering through the fierce June heat were fulfilling their role, and being as honest as they always were, since it would have been simple for them to disappear in the general confusion.

The notes end there, but there is a small satin purse with a note in Maria's handwriting, "This little bag I picked up in our curtained off room in the Fort of Phillour (Punjab) the day I left for Simla in such peril in June'57" So no dramatic crinolined trek down to Delhi, but a retreat to the hills where she stayed safely until October. All the action was further south, and neither of them suffered further alarms though there was still plenty going on, as Maria informed her uncle Luxmore in Devon when she rejoined Juxon in Ambala.

This is the first of Maria's letters to survive, written when she was twenty seven, and it reflected the views of most of the British at the time. Given her frightening experience in Phillaur and the continuing uneasy state of the country, her savage tone can be partly forgiven.

"I had such a bad report (about Juxon) that I set off from Simla immediately, and came down as fast as I could and arrived two days ago having left my precious darling children behind. It was a dreadful trip, parting for the first time with my children and not knowing how I would find my own dear Henry, but by God's grace he was all right on my arrival which took him quite by surprise. I was expecting him on leave and thought we should both go back to Simla immediately, but he could not possibly get away so I must rejoice that I came down. My darlings come down next week, under a good Ayah's charge, and we are longing to have them with us. We go into their little rooms which are ready for them and look at the three little beds and Minnie's armchairs and table with such longing to have our pets. Mrs Trench is taking care of them and she writes daily and tells me how they are which is a very great comfort. I am so very happy now I am back with dear Henry and we are living in Cantonments again in such a comfortable house. We are all in wonder and indignation at the apathy of the English government in not sending out troops, if they would only believe our terrible and great danger they would be more active. If Delhi had not fallen when it did Sir. J. Lawrence said he could not have held the Punjab another week. We were in the greatest peril, Lucknow was only relieved by General Havelock a few days ago and today a telegraph message tells of a great fight at Agra. One of the rebels attacked them suddenly on all sides, and after a struggle we thoroughly routed them and took all their guns. The King of Delhi is a prisoner. Even now the eyes of all are not open and Lord Canning who ought to be turned out of India is behaving so ridiculously and leniently that the rebels are not punished, by and by when you hear all the horrors committed you will wish tortures could be invented to punish the wretches in this country. On entering Delhi we found a man supposed to be a villain crucified in the palace, another tied down like a horse and cut evidently with hot swords all over. Can you fancy anything so horrible? Yet the king is spared. Some of his sons have been killed. A European sergeant of the 2nd Grenadiers has been assisting them in Delhi all these months, and was caught with the king's sons and hung. Too good a death for him." The end of the letter is missing, which is just as well.

The last letter on the subject was written a year later in 1858, also to Uncle Luck. Things had settled down, Bertram had been born and little Eleanor was not yet dead, she died at three years old, a seemingly unlamented child. "Our regiment is behaving very well I am thankful to say and I am quite reconciled to them going about armed again" Maria wrote. Of course Juxon did not actually belong to any particular regiment, but was attached to whoever needed his services. Then there is a six year gap, and when the family surfaces again Willie, Irene, Annie my grandmother and Tom have been added, with Flo and Beatrice in the wings. And importantly for Maria, Uncle Tom has appeared on the scene, a cavalry officer who moved into the Jones household, and I suspect into Maria's heart, while fifty-one year old Juxon. tubby and balding, tutored his eldest son, played unaccompanied on his fiddle, and though he got close enough to her to father two more children, is never mentioned in his wife's letters.

The family seem now to have settled in Ambala, the main military station of the north, and would be living the life of comfort and ease of their kind. With plenty of servants, a club, and regimental parties to attend, cantonments were lively places in the winter. In the heat of summer they moved up into the hills in Kasauli, later to become the centre of the Pasteur Institute and the repository of the brains of mad dogs, but in their day a cool retreat where much the same life was enjoyed. Here four of the children - Minnie, Berty, Willie and Coco (Irene) were sent away from home to start their education in the home of a family called Vice. They were taught by the unmarried sister of Mr Vice which could hardly have been an enlivening experience, and the idea would have been to keep them occupied and out of the plains. Harry stayed at home and was taught by Juxon, who worked harder at this than anything else, until Harry was fifteen and they retired.

Maria wrote to Kasauli when she wasn't on hand to keep an eye on them. She was anxious about their contacts. "I shall be very glad when all those boys are off" she told Minnie, referring it seems to other pupils, "for not being gentlemen I particularly dislike your mixing with them. It was good of that little Harry giving you those nice presents but remember he is not of your own rank and so I should not like you to be seen mixing with him and the others and they can do you no good and on the contrary harm.". What harm did she envisage? The wrong accent perhaps but this was a much greater danger when Minnie was sent to school in Simla and there were girls of mixed blood, the result of the many unions between British officers and Indian women.

Minnie was thirteen when she was sent to Holly Lodge, a school in Simla started and run by a Miss Mackinnon. After she left the school moved to the spacious ex government house built for Lord Auckland, and in fact still exists there. It upped its image and standards, teachers were trained and often brought from England, and one headmistress was a prestigious lady from Cheltenham Lady's College. But Holly Lodge was a modest house, a dark, damp flat roofed building in which Minnie was homesick, cold, and troubled with toothache and chilblains.   A smattering of History (English) Literature and Maths was on the menu, but more useful subjects like embroidery, dancing and music took up most of the school day.

Maria with her three eldest daughters, Eastbourne 1874

Minnie howled for weeks on end, but her mother reproved her "my darling you must try and not give way to crying. I know and feel deeply how unhappy you are my own child, but darling all girls nearly have to go to school and believe me it is for your own good and you would have deeply regretted growing up

71

ignorant my child." She was more concerned about the usual dangers of meeting the wrong people. "Don't kiss Mrs Byrne or let her kiss you" she shrilly warned her daughter about the dusky matron. "I would just as soon you kissed the Mehta." This was the sweeper, the lowest and dirtiest of the servants, and it seemed that something in saliva was polluting. Miss Mackinnon had to employ Eurasian women, as no "decent" lady would have done the job, especially not for the money she offered.

At first Maria exhorted her homesick daughter to pull herself together. Finally she refused to answer Minnie's tearful effusions. "You must try to bear your sorrow more bravely, for Mama's sake you must be a good grateful child and not distress me with your sad letters" she ordered, and finally "You are upsetting me most deeply with your great sorrow and for this reason I cannot write to you any more my dearest child until you have conquered your homesickness and settled down and so no more letters from Mama old girl until you cease from your troubles my darling child, dear old Pins." Settling down was what all children of the Raj had to do, for fear of upsetting their elders.

So settle Minnie finally did, putting up with toothache and chilblains and being examined by the matron in a way that frightened and embarrassed her, though how this was achieved without being touched must have caused extra problems. She put up with walks in crocodiles along Simla's dripping hill paths, and having her best friend die of dysentery. So her mother started to write to her again with her own particular worries. "I very much hope that the other girls are ladies. As for those who are dark, ignore them. It is a sad fact that unions are made in India between the nicest of men of the best families, and women of no breeding who have coloured forbears. The sad result we must simply accept as part of God's plan but there is no need either to speak or even have physical contact with these poor creatures. I know Mama can trust you not to have such a girl as a close friend or a friend of any kind." God who had filled the world with snakes and cockroaches and coloured people would not ask the impossible of the Joneses. He was, by implication, as racist and snobbish as they were.

When Minnie got a letter from a young officer she had met in Ambala another danger loomed. A special runner was sent up the hillside to express Maria's horror. "I hope you do not on any account mention having had the letter. If the young fool is at Umballa he will get more than he likes from Uncle Tom." The letter had been intercepted and read by Miss Mackinnon and its contents forwarded. Minnie got very few, if any, love letters in her life, and it seems she never even got the chance to read this one.

By this time Uncle Tom had become the centre of Maria's life, his name mentioned in every letter. He was a Captain in a cavalry regiment, Tom Wright, eventually a General. three times married but never for some reason to Maria. When he was stationed at Ambala he had a room in their bungalow, when not he spent all his leaves with them. Maria was thirty-six but still attractive though thin and pale after fourteen years in India. Tom was tall and handsome; he had fought at Chillianwallah and in the North West frontier, and his comings and goings, dressed to kill, were a contrast to sedentary, tubby little Juxon.

It must have been a bit galling to Minnie in her damp banishment to hear of her mother's life of parties, always attended by Uncle Tom. There was one lunch for instance. "Colonel Denis dined here and Mrs Arbuthnot came after dinner and they had such fun pretending my little round pillow was her baby and every now and then pretending it was crying, when she was singing she pretended to throw a book at Uncle Tom and then she chased him round the room." They had all drunk a lot of wine which probably made it seem funnier than it sounds. There were gymkhanas, pig sticking, and paper chases. Uncle Tom provided Maria with a horse and she wrote to Minnie of exhilarating gallops "I was a few yards in front of Uncle Tom's regiment, and they suddenly began to gallop in, I had to gallop too just in front of them and I did not mind it in the slightest. There were plenty of people in parade looking on." Nobody seemed surprised at this mother of seven charging about on the parade ground. Whether Juxon minded is never revealed.

When it grew hot in Ambala they moved up to Kasauli where there were excitements to report. "One of the Asylum boys came to the compound a few days ago where somebody lived, we gave him a slice of bread and cheese in the garden, but in he marched into the house and the boys just stopped him coming where we were having tiffin. Afterwards he did not go away but will you believe it in the afternoon when I was undressed and lying down he walked right into my bedroom and we could not get rid of him until Uncle Tom ordered him away. Well 2 days after without our knowing he was there, he came straight into the dressing room, Harry pushed him out and shut the door. He joined four other boys outside, and they said they would not go away. Berty chased them down the road and knocked the boy down and left him crying."

There were a lot of orphans in India who were housed in cheerless "asylums" in a haphazard but well meaning way. Emma Roberts in her travels described these institutions, bad enough for the boys, worse for the girls who, when they reached a marriageable age were put up for auction and claimed as brides by private soldiers. Since they were usually "coloured" they felt lucky that anyone would have them. The orphan boys who invaded Maria's house sound like stray dogs, longing for a proper home and the constant affection of a permanent owner.

Maria's party going was temporarily suspended when she complained to Minnie "very little upsets me now". She was pregnant with Flo, her ninth living child, destined to be a scourge to my mother, a delight to the concert goers of Deal, Maria's prop in old age, a lifelong support through her will to my grandmother, a warning to me of the dangers of constipation, a light in the eyes of a Major Pilleau. She arrived without trouble on December 8th 1867. Very soon afterwards a real tragedy hit the family and brought forward their retirement from India

73

On September 16th 1868 there arrived for Minnie in Simla the first of several black edged letters. These brought to her the news of the death of her brother, little Tom, the first of three little boys whose deaths were to become a plaintive chorus of never ending sorrow. Her mother's shrieks as she got the news of little Glen's death were the first clear memory of my mother. She mourned her little Monty for sixty years, and worried about the weeds on his far away grave until her own death healed the wound at last.

Tom, a beautiful near four year old, whose sayings and doings his mother often described in her letters, died within twelve hours of what sounds like diphtheria. Sudden deaths of small children were a commonplace in India, Juxon's medical skills had failed before and could do nothing now for his son. They all had to sit round helplessly watching the child toss in pain, and then collapse into a coma. By a strange coincidence I read the letters describing his death on September the 14th, the day it happened.

It was a day his family kept like a saint's day afterwards, taking out his hair (which is still bright and shining in an envelope) cut from his cold brow, lighting candles and remembering their "angel in heaven". His father mourned him most I think, perhaps a lonely man with Maria's affections drifting in other directions. Years later my grandmother opened one of his books and found on a piece of paper in his handwriting " I will go to him." It wasn't long in fact before they were reunited.

Minnie in her banishment must have found the letters hard to bear. "The darling had had a cold" Maria wrote, "but that was all, and on Saturday we went to the soldiers' gardens. Our darling will be buried this evening, very soon to part with his dear body. This time yesterday our pet was playing outside with the children. Oh Pins, my darling I know how deeply you will feel this blow, almost as much as we (Papa and I) do. The children were all round the bed when our darling's spirit fled. Thank God for the last hour he was insensible for all through his sufferings he was conscious. He could not speak for hours but once when I put my ear to his lips seeing he wanted to speak said "I feel very ill." Last night he asked to be undressed and then he said his prayers. His speaking of them was very difficult so I said them for him aloud. He had lately always said them by himself, always beginning with "Amen" strangely."

Next day she elaborated. "No words of mine could describe the heavenly beauty of Tom's face after his death. It was glorious, such as must be seen to be imagined. It increased every hour until as each of us went in turn to look at our boy, we asked the other if we noticed the increasing beauty of the precious face. The smile was heavenly and the whole face radiant. It seemed to have a message of love for me as I looked at it. I kissed him for you my child, so deeply feeling that you could not have the privilege my darling. Today I think of him as a blessed angel in his Father's arms, looking at us all I do not doubt and if he could would he not urge us all to live so as to meet him again? Let us my own Pins henceforth try to follow where our darling has gone before. I have a treasure there now. He is forever saying "Sun of my soul my Saviour dear, it is not night if thou art near" and those two lines we have ordered to be put on his tombstone which is ordered from Delhi by Uncle Tom. You know I never let him buy a godfather's present for our little one and now he says he feels he should much like to do this for our lost darling. He often spoke of you my darling, it was so sudden his end that I feel now if I could have him for a short time more and make much of him I should be happy."

That last sentence rings bitterly true. Try as she would to turn him into an angel it was the flesh and blood little boy she longed for, whom she may have scolded and sent to his death unforgiven. This second letter tries to beatify him, her third goes through the next stage of grief, the pain of the little reminders of his life. "I look through his dear clothes till my heart is ready to break with anguish. His dear boots, and his little socks pushed in them, taken off on Saturday night, I took today from under his bed. On Sunday he wore shoes and I cut his nails at his own request as he lay playing on my lap. I took his dear clothes from the dhobi, how I feel having to give out two sheets and two pillow cases less. On Saturday I gave the dersy cloth for six shirts for him, and in the evening I found one ready. Little did I think what it would be for. He was buried in it, and on Monday afternoon some clothes came here for him. Pins darling as I said before, let us so live that we may rejoin our lost darling."

Thirteen year old Harry wrote too. "Poor little fellow, he was playing on Sunday so happily. In the middle of the day he went to sleep and about tiffin time he woke up half strangled, then Uncle Tom took him to Papa and Papa put some iodine on his neck and gave him some medicine, we bathed his dear little feet in warm water and then put him on my bed, he then got a little well and in the evening he called Papa to call Lora to take his clothes off, then Mama Papa and Uncle Tom went to dinner and I stayed by his side, after dinner we went in to see how he was and found him in great distress, about that time he said "my prayers", Papa said I will call Mama to say them to you, he always when he said them began with "Amen" so Mama did the same, Uncle Tom had the couch placed by his bedside and he was placed on it, poor little darling he bore it so well he was rolling from one side of the bed to the other he could not keep still on account of his sufferings. He was then put on Uncle Tom's bed and he began breathing so violently poor blessed little darling, towards the morning he began to be very pale and insensible, it was half past four when Paoa wrote for the doctors but they could do nothing when they came, the last words he said were "my milk and water" - at half past eight the blessed little angel died, we all came round him and we all cried very much for him and all the servants too. Papa put our poor little brother's body at the foot of the bed for the whole day, when his little coffin came and then he was put in it for the night, but was not shut up till next morning, we all kissed the dear dead body and shut it up never to see it again, he was buried on Tuesday morning, the Vices came to the funeral."

This letter from "backward" Harry brought that long ago death so vividly before me that it didn't seem a hundred and fifty years since little Tom tossed in pain with iodine stains on his neck. My grandmother who was five at the time forgot his dying, but remembered that once when they were teasing him he had said haughtily "All right, I'm going to God then" a remark they later recalled with guilty gloom. She and I often sang his favourite hymn "Sun of my soul" as we knelt by her brocade sofa in Notting Hill Gate.

Two days after the death Uncle Tom wrote a stiff little note. "This is now the second morning since your dear little brother left us, but his sweet little musical voice appears to be still ringing in our ears and every moment one half expects to see him running into the room with his wonted impetuosity to announce in his emphatic language some occurrence among his brothers and sisters." I have wondered whether Uncle Tom was more than a godfather, given the many occasions that he and Maria were alone together on rides and returning from dances and parties. There are no pictures of him to ponder likenesses.

Juxon took four days to write. "I have only just now thrown away the flowers which I gathered in the soldiers' garden on Saturday when little Tom was running about amongst the flower beds with me. Only think of his having died and withered long before these frail flowers. Mama will desire to read what I write to you my dear child so I must avoid as much as possible all allusions that would tend to renew her sorrow. His toy horse is the thing most associated with the dear little fellow and so Uncle Tom and we are going to keep part of it."

How unhealthy these Victorian rituals now appear, how morbid the idea of children gathering round their dead brother and kissing his brow, how slightly grotesque the idea of carving up a hobby horse and dividing the pieces like some primitive tribe sharing the sacred relics. My mother remembered it as a treat of her childhood to be allowed to play with another sanctified steed, that of little Glen. She had never known this dead brother of hers since she was still in Burma, nor at the time did she know how much more affection was given to his horse than to him in his lifetime.

Minnie's reactions to the stream of sad letters flowing to her from her family that September are only expressed in one letter when she suggested that baby Flo had been sent by God as a substitute for Tom, an idea for which her mother thanked her but in which she didn't find much comfort. Berty and Willie were the only members of the family who seemed unmoved, one more bitter mark against them. At ten and nine the whole business of kissing corpses must have been chilling and embarrassing. It could even have crossed their minds that they would have been less missed.

Tom's death brought their life in India to an end. They had been thinking of retiring, considered and abandoned the idea of Tasmania, and Uncle Tom on leave organised the purchase of a house in Eastbourne. In the following spring they packed up and left, with what feelings is not divulged in any letter. My grandmother Annie was six and told me of the long sea trip home when she spent a lot of time being amused by the crew. She and Harry were the only ones who were to return East.

In Eastbourne when her dancing days were over, Maria must have looked back longingly to her cantonment life. As the grey mists rolled in she would have recalled the beguiling spicy airs of Ambala, through which she had ridden with her handsome cavalry officer. Listening to the band on the promenade was no substitute for mess nights, the blaze and glitter of uniforms, the white flutter of servants, tropical moons, the scent of jasmine, the non-stop clink of glasses filled with all the drinks that poured through Indian days and nights.

I really don't know what she felt because from then on she was silent, picked up again as a handsome imperious old lady, long widowed and living in London with her two unmarried daughters Minnie and Flo. Straight backed and still beautiful, the last portrait of her is hard to reconcile with the flinger of cushions and the fearless rider of cavalry chargers. The negative feelings I have towards her stem partly from my mother's accounts of the "barneys" in Palace Mansions and Drayton Gardens. My mother disliked her, thought her selfish and domineering. My cousin George said she was a typical Juxon Jones, an erratic, bad tempered lot. Flawed maybe, but there are excuses. Did she grow to resent the marriage plans that linked her for life with a man she never loved? Who knows. She was trapped like all the women of her time, and sprung the same traps for her daughters, who in turn arranged the cages round theirs. This her great granddaughter was the last to beat her head against the bars.

ANNIE AND HER SISTERS: GRANDMOTHER AND GREAT-AUNTS

Seated left to right: Harry, Medora Hulke, Irene, Annie with Glen on her lap.
Standing left to right: Florence, Federick Hulke – son and father, Minnie.

I have a file stuffed with papers labelled "The Eastbourne House", and photographs and paintings of it, 13 Lushington Terrace. It was an imposing square mansion, set in stately gardens, probably picked up for a song in 1869 when my great grand-parents Juxon and Maria moved into it.

In a letter written to Minnie in Simla, Juxon discussed his retirement plans, but his ideas then were centred on Cheltenham. First thoughts of Tasmania had been put aside because "the means of educating the girls were very inadequate." The boys would have had farming and cattle rearing to occupy them, but he had heard that the population was decreasing "with a dearth of farming and domestic servants." There was also the problem of "a very disagreeable twang" which would grate on Jones ears.

"So now Pins " he wrote "you may picture to yourself your living in Cheltenham one of the smartest, dearest most gay and cheerful towns in England." where many old friends were to be found and easily accessible by rail to his sisters. Minnie must have been much cheered by the prospect of a move to such a place from Miss Mackinnon's dreary establishment. I don't know why they settled instead for Eastbourne, perhaps the good schools, particularly its Ladies College.

The Eastbourne house was where Beatrice was born, Juxon died, my grandmother grew up, Coco eloped from, Maria upped and left from in a huff when she overheard a remark about "those Jones girls". It finally became one of the main sources of income for my grandmother, and received a direct hit in the war, and so the subject of endless correspondence about compensation. It was eventually rebuilt as two flats and there was talk of my parents going there when they retired but they disliked the idea. In the end it was sold for a "pittance" which irked my mother for years.

Great-aunt Minnie

Minnie was sixteen when they settled in Eastbourne, attractive, tall and slim like her mother. She would soon be putting up her hair and coming out into society to meet suitable young men. Yet things went wrong for her. The three boys seem to have taken up most of the family's time, and when they were finally sorted out and dispatched east and west, the three younger sisters were blossoming into prospective brides. She was unlucky in her place in the family, followed by three brothers; there were seven years between her and a sister. The iron had cooled considerably by the time her case could be considered, and couldn't be struck for suitors. The shelf life for spinsters was short.

My grandmother remembered the Eastbourne house as a rather gloomy place with Papa in pain (he suffered terribly from neuralgia in the damp sea air) and Mama strict, into which came one blessed day a young nurse. Nurse took the baby Beatrice from birth, and gave her and the three youngest children all the fun, warmth and love they needed. They lived the life of the upstairs nursery, with visits to the drawing room after tea, and it was made happy for them by Nurse. She was spoken for but she couldn't leave her charges, and delayed her marriage for ten years, until the time Maria took umbrage and transferred the family to London, changing their name to Juxon Jones at the same time.

Then she and her Fred were married, but too late to have children of their own, and the marriage was a short one. Fred worked in a cotton mill and his lungs filled with fluff, and after six years his fluff filled lungs gave out and he died. Nurse retired to a tiny cottage in Rutland and was helped with spasmodic donations from Drayton Gardens. My grandmother was still visiting her when I was a child, now just Poor Old Nurse eking out her last years in the poverty expected of her.

Juxon found that in spite of all his hard work, Harry still hadn't reached the standards required by the Civil Service, and he joined the Indian Army, where his skill with guns and horses served him well. The luckless pair Berty and Willie were sent to school and then despatched to the New World. My mother read letters describing Berty's journey to New South Wales "before the mast", but she said they were so sad that she destroyed them. He died at the age of thirty four in Ararat, Victoria, of pneumonia according to the local paper. The marble tombstone sent out by his "devoted mother" would have cost more than the return passage he begged for. Willy went to Canada and disappeared from sight for many years to no ones apparent concern.

The girls went to Eastbourne Ladies College for a year or two each. They all showed signs of a rare beauty which must have been a great relief to Maria, lining them up for the marriage market. Suffragettes were much frowned on by the Joneses who didn't recognise their tempestuous rows as a sign of frustration and boredom. The first of them to get married, Irene or Coco, did it in an exciting way by eloping, quite why my mother couldn't explain, since her husband Frederick Hulke was a doctor and she was twenty-seven. The Joneses only married into the professions if possible, and Fred's was obviously a reasonable one.

However romantic their beginnings, when they emerge into family snapshots it is as a prosperous pair living in Admiralty House in Deal, complete with carriage and a red yacht in the bay. My mother spent holidays with them as a girl, and nothing could have been more sedate than their lifestyle, Coco a busty matron much given to amateur dramatics. The news of her stage successes were pasted into her sister Minnie's album, the "Deal Walmer and Sandwich Mercury" was ecstatic about her. For the big concert of the year the "London contingent" came down (Minnie and Flo) to play and sing alongside. Yearly she and a Mr Metcalfe brought down the house with their performance of "Where are you going to my pretty maid?". "She was charming" enthused the paper "and the air of gracefulness and freedom which she assumed would have done credit to professional talent." They also enthused about Flo's skill with a violin, her beauty and ability to please.

Great-aunt Coco

Graceful is not the word that springs to mind when considering Coco. In the photographs of early in the century she appears weighed down by an enormous bust and hat. By then she was a middle aged matron referred to by my mother in her diary as The Beast, though like most of Violet's nicknames it exaggerated. She lectured a lot and "made" Violet break off her first engagement. On the other hand she worked hard for Destitute Children and local poor boatmen. To raise money for these she opened Admiralty House for fancy dress balls, and "The Mercury" was there to write up the costumes. Minnie always appeared as a Dresden shepherdess, one of the delightful outfits "donned by the fair sex" said the Mercury, who also enthused about the "splendid repasts" provided.

There were a lot of wounded soldiers in Deal during the war, and Coco helped to bandage them, but she didn't invite them to her tennis parties. In between good works the Hulke household was often rent by "rows" and "bust ups", so it seems Coco was Flawed, and with Harry living down the road and the visits of the "London contingent" at regular intervals, it was lucky they lived in large houses with thick walls. Coco had two children one of whom, Medora, my mother was fond of and kept in touch with. By a strange coincidence a great grandson turned up as my driving instructor.

Great-aunt Beatrice

There was never any doubt that Beatrice would marry because she was always referred to as The Beautiful and this in a family of singular good looks. She wed at nineteen, a rich diamond merchant from Argentina. Fred Crowther's vowels were suspect and being in Trade was a pity, but the mother of five daughters couldn't be too fussy. She was married in Buenos Aires where Maria's brother was the bishop, and what happened next my mother was vague about, but five years later Beatrice was back for good with two little girls. Not long afterwards Fred conveniently died and left her to play for many years the role of rich and beautiful widow. Men were constantly in attendance at her flat in Hyde Park Mansions, but my mother thought there was something in Fred's will about the money stopping if she remarried.

Beatrice was all that my mother admired; idle, frivolous and spendthrift. She never sang for destitute children, Deal was far too dull for her. She drove round in one of the first cars, dressed in fur coats, rode her own horse in Rotten Row and entertained lavishly. Her presents rescued birthdays; white skates, silk blouses, jewellery, they shine out of my mother's diaries among the handkerchiefs and writing pads. She was gracious, confident and much admired, revelling without worries in a "good time". Violet worshipped her as a model, and spent a lot of her life trying to emulate her.

And then Beatrice's good times ended. She suddenly ran out of money, unaware that even large amounts of capital come to an end. Spending money was all that Beatrice knew about it, a vulgar subject anyway, never discussed in the family. So out went the cars and furs, the horse, the furniture. Beatrice drifted about between boarding houses, her last address in Lancaster Gate, rooms she shared with her sadly disturbed daughter Aileen whose story comes later. She died in her early sixties of pneumonia, a foolish but seemingly unflawed Jones girl.

Grand-mother Annie

Annie at the time of her marriage

Annie was the last of the family to marry, and the only one for whom her mother Maria had to provide a society wedding. Annie was six when her parents retired to Eastbourne. The sharpest memory of her childhood was of the jangle of bells when Juxon slumped in his chair of a heart attack six years later. She went to the Ladies College and then at twenty two, with Flo, to the Conservatoire at Brussels to learn the violin. In old age she spoke of sexual harassment from the father of the family they boarded with, perhaps nothing out of the ordinary. She was removed rather hastily when she got engaged to a Belgian. There were limits as to how foreign you could be to marry a Jones.

On her return she met Rodway Swinhoe, a solicitor on leave from Calcutta, and they quickly became engaged, but because of complications over his father's estate, couldn't marry for five years. My grandmother often showed me a ring he gave her, five diamonds in the shape of the plough constellation which he used to look at in Burma where he had gone, and she in Drayton Gardens though the skies there were often clouded and starless. To fill in the time of waiting Annie went out to Buenos Aires to stay with her uncle the Bishop; Waite Stirling who was the first Bishop of the Falkland Islands.

One letter survives from Annie in Argentina, dated April 22nd 1887, and tells of an excursion to Mendoza. "One saloon compartment was set aside for unmarried ladies in which was a large sleeping compartment, one smaller one and 2 lavatories. The bachelors had another carriage to themselves and several carriages were reserved for married people. We were 16 altogether - the Pakenhams being of our party. We had a special train, it was arranged that we should never travel by night which was a comfort. Tea was brought to our saloon in the morning and we breakfasted at 12 (according to the custom of the country) always managing to reach some station or other for this meal or dinner. At Villa Mercedes four carriages were awaiting us, and we drove all round the town, went down to the river where we chased butterflies, grasshoppers etc. The natives came flocking to their doors with bewildered faces staring unmercifully at us." Less pretty were the macabre remains of the earthquake of 1861 when an estimated twenty five thousand people were buried alive. Bones, skulls and teeth were still to be picked up as souvenirs.

Minor mishaps occurred on the train. Miss Smith was taken ill with suspected cholera and Mr Wilkinson's manservant fell out of a window during the night. This news was telegraphed further up the line without comment as to his injuries; servants were notoriously careless. The special train, the segregation of the sexes, the servants, reminded me of our pampered travel across India in the days of the Raj. In those palmy times Viceroys had bands waiting for them at stations, to play "My love is but a lassie yet" and "Auld Land Syne".

My mother never ceased to be cross with Annie for going to Buenos Aires when she was already engaged; Flo should have gone and found herself a husband there. The one already supplied by Argentina had not been a great success admittedly but the Bishop would move in the right company and have nothing to do with Trade. It was another year before Annie and her Rodway reached the altar, when they were both twenty six. It was a grand wedding reported as far afield as New York, and was followed by a honeymoon in Paris. "Rodway and I do something enjoyable every day" wrote Annie to her mother, "In the morning we visit some picture gallery or some well known place of interest, in the afternoon we always have ices, and finish the day with either a drive in the Bois or a theatre." Rodway gave her a paste buckle which she said shone like diamonds. I have it and it looks like paste to me. How envious were Minnie and Flo I wonder, sitting with Mother with not a suitor in sight.

After Paris came Burma, to which she was despatched with the same carefree relief as other Victorian girls of the time. Did Maria have memories of her arrival in the tropics, her two dead babies, the unreliable natives, the killing climate? It seems not, or perhaps she thought Burma was different. When I stayed with her as a child my grandmother described it as a picture book country of golden pagodas and red palaces, of streams full of sacred fish, of orchids and emeralds, amber and jade, of lovely laughing carefree people.. In a bungalow outside the town walls of Mandalay she and Rodway began the life that contented them for thirty eight years. A couple of hours away was the new hill station of Maymyo, where Rodway laid out gardens, and in its cool pine scented air was born my mother, and later her son William.

Annie loved Burma, but created in it the life of Eastbourne and Drayton Gardens. She went calling with visiting cards, gloved and hatted. After dinner parties she played the violin as well as she had learnt it at Brussels, and sang the ballads that had so entranced the people of Deal. Every year she broke off her social life to have a baby; Lawrence, Margery, Glen, Bertram, and Violet. With each of these she grew a little stouter but remained beautiful, her skin protected by veils, which she continued to wear even when I knew her in London.

Rodway wrote poems which were published in the Rangoon Times.

> Careless, remote, a land of rest
> Where there are found no slaves by toil oppressed,
> No fretful nation yearning to be free,
> But golden rivers glinting by the sea.

Cocooned and contented, they had no idea of what was really going on in the country, and when the Prince of Wales paid them a visit in 1922 they thought everyone was as delighted as they were to welcome him. Annie's letter describing this event is worth quoting in full.

"Our beloved Prince left last night" she wrote to her brother Harry's daughter Babs. "and we are all feeling very flat and its difficult to believe that all the excitement of his visit is gone not to return. He is just adorable, and when one curtsies gives one the most delicious smile. Well to begin with there was the Reception at the Station for which everyone had tickets and seats, and where various men were presented to HRH. A speech was made first in Burmese to which the Prince replied. The next day at 8 was parade and we all had to be on the Parade Ground before 7.30. We were quite close to HRH. After this Violet, Winifred and I started the decoration of 50 small and various large tables. The flowers were beautiful, but the heat dried them poor dears, in the afternoon, but the whole effect was beautiful and the tea most excellent. These decorations were for a Polo At Home given in honour of HRH. The Prince came down in the morning for a practice. He was due to arrive at 4 at the At Home but he came at 3.30 and played a most excellent game and his team won the match so carried away a lovely cup and when Lady Craddock gave it to him he said it was "much too good". There was a splendid tent for him to have tea and there were four tables and I was to have been at one with some of HRH's staff but HRH would not come till all tea was over so I had it alone with Mrs Thornton and the Vice President of the club's wife. We spent our time cheering him. I was dining at G.H. that night so dashed home to dress and so did Violet and to our sorrow we heard that the Prince without ceremony strolled into the Club Bar just as if he were an ordinary member. Will was there and fetched the Visitor's Book and got him to write in it and also to sign a picture of himself which the club has which the Prince said was a horrid picture and he would send another. Will came home with eyes fairly dancing with delight.

You can imagine my excitement at the dinner party. First we all assembled in the drawing room, then Lady Craddock and the Lt.Governor came in and shook hands with us. We were all lined up with the man who was to take us in and we waited and various members of the staff came and then one announced his Royal Highness and then Sir Reginald introduced us in turn by name and we curtsied and the Prince shook hands and then we trooped into dinner and I was on the left of the Lt.Governor and just opposite the Prince. He has the most adorable face and looks a baby. He is very strong willed and is always upsetting arrangements, which he considers foolish, in little things. At dinner he seemed to eat nothing but his own little pile of biscuit bread and Lady Craddock said he was always cutting down the menu and I noticed several things were cut off the menu. The ADC told us that everything was going to be very informal and that after dessert smokes would be brought in and that HRH would rise and lead Lady Craddock into the drawing room where we would all follow and have coffee. On reaching the drawing room HRH went over to where his polo cup was and Lady Fane, Mrs Thornton and I followed and we chatted about the cup. It was arranged that the Prince should disappear and that we were all to go off to the entertainment at the Shan Camp, but HRH chose to sit on so Lord Cromer told us to go and as I passed him I bobbed and he gave me a bow as I turned on the landing and I gave him my best curtsey. Yesterday was the Garden Party and we were constantly near him and yelling or rather cheering ourselves hoarse according to directions. The departure was private but quite a lot of people were there to see him off at 7.30 p.m. I used darling Mother's parasol at the Garden Party and it caused quite a sensation and was so sweet and Will came and congratulated me on my appearance which was most encouraging. Well darling I hope all this will interest you and if you think old nurse would like to read it send it along to her."

This absurdly obsequious letter was treasured by the family, and I daresay my grandmother read it over many times in her tiny flat in London, wondering at the past which had supplied Princes and Lords for her to dine with and curtsey to. The picture that emerges is of a spoilt and thoughtless young man, upsetting arrangements, refusing food prepared by special cooks brought in for the occasion. My mother's memory of the Prince was of a small man in a suit who looked insignificant beside the bronzed and feathered tribal chiefs of Burma. My father recalled the Prince going out of his way to upset everyone, dancing with "little chi chi girls" instead of the Governor's Lady. It fitted the attitude to royalty of the time though. When I stayed with my grandmother in Notting Hill Gate we would scan the Morning Post daily to see where Their Majesties were going to be that day, and if possible go there to catch a glimpse of them. The sight of a gloved hand at a window would send us home glowing.

By returning East, the only Jones girl to do so, Annie unwittingly started the sad trail of children home. She went back to see her family at three yearly intervals, Rodway only once during their growing up. In 1910 she took her eldest daughter Margery back to Burma with her to marry her off. They had a memorable journey described in a letter to Violet, six years younger and left at home. "I expect Margery has told you of our exciting day at Port Said and how we missed the steamer and had to take the train to Suez. It will be a nightmare always seeing the Big Steamer getting further and further away and our own panting motor boat making no way at all." They had been strolling about, shopping and eating ices, when they "saw to our horror the Warwickshire was moving. We were beside ourselves and urged our boatman to row harder. Seeing it was useless we signalled to a passing motor boat and climbed in but though we went at full speed the Warwickshire gradually got smaller and smaller and the men said it was useless and turned the boat to Port Said." Fortunately there was a train up to Suez, the journey enlivened when "at one station a third class passenger died and was carried past our carriage." They caught the boat next morning, mightily relieved, one of the hazards being that the Manager of the Ruby Mines in Burma was with them and had to be left alone with Margery some of the time; a man with a Reputation alone with an unmarried girl was not nice at all, even though they were surrounded by a couple of hundred Egyptians on a busy street.

The Burma idyll ended suddenly in 1927 when Rodway had a small stroke. He was taken to hospital to rest, and seemed cheerful, joking with everyone as usual. Then he said "I'm so tired" and turned over and died. He was sixty four, and so was Annie, not an easy age to leave huge bungalows surrounded by acres of gardens, waited on by strings of servants, for a fifth floor flat in Notting Hill

Gate. She lived for another twenty-nine years, giving me for two or three of them a sandalwood-scented solace to which in dreams I still return.

Three out of five daughters married was a good average but for the two who didn't make it to the altar life was cheerless. Minnie and Flo, both beautiful and talented, drew the short straws in the family. Maria decided to lay herself out on her ottoman when she was in her fifties, and be an interesting ailing widow like her sovereign. First Minnie, then when she died Flo, fitted the slot of unmarried daughter whose role it was to tend her. Minnie only seemed to have one tenuous love affair, with a man who wrote her appalling poetry which she pasted in her album. He not only had a wife but died when he was thirty nine. Minnie herself died in 1902 at forty-nine, and my mother remembered her last pain filled days, when she lay on a sofa and little Violet held up a hand to shelter her from the heat of the fire. She was buried in Kensal Green cemetery on an April day that was kept sacred by the Joneses, my mother making ritual pilgrimages to the grave in her teens.

Then Flo had to take over Maria, who lasted another ten years. She was thirty three, and for reasons not explained hadn't married a Captain Pilleau. His baritone voice had also enchanted Deal, and he continued to trail after Flo until he was a Major, but then got himself killed in the first year of the war. When my mother knew Flo she was a bitter bad-tempered woman, devoted to only one thing, her dog Donald. When Violet was thirteen her aunt took her into her bedroom and told her that there were five letters concealed under paper in the bottom drawer of her dressing table. If she died suddenly Violet was to go straight to the drawer and destroy them. What tender secrets were concealed in Flo's Five Letters? How typical that she had to keep them from the prying eyes of her mother. Reading one's children's private correspondence, even when they were middle aged women, was a common Victorian pastime.

My mother often talked of the "blazing rows" at Drayton Gardens, Flo letting off the head of steam of one more Flawed Jones. Two months after Major Pilleau's death she set off for Burma to join her sister Annie in a land where men were many and desperate for brides. She was forty seven and her chances, even in the East, were only fair. "She made a fool of herself, painting her face and chasing every man in sight" said my mother. She returned to work in a wartime hospital in Devon but died quite soon, attended by her brother Harry who described her last illness as being very painful, probably cancer. The story in the family was that it was the result of a week without Going, a distant feat of constipation which probably prompted my mother to dose us with Castor Oil once a week.

I think of Minnie pasting into her album those awful poems of her only admirer, and then on a page to itself the notice of his death. And then I think of the Simla school, teeth aching, chilblains burning, best friends dying, and of the Eastbourne house where nobody came to woo, and I wonder if, like the two little dead girls before her, it would have been better if she had failed to take a first breath. And Flo, who dazzled Deal, fading away her fiddle unplayed, no outlet for her talents, no jobs available that a "lady" could do, tied to a tiresome old semi invalid who she had to pretend to love. Of all Maria's daughters my grandmother Annie was the most blessed, happily married and noticeably free of the Flaw. The only thing she did wrong was to go back East, where my mother and I had to follow her and from where we had to send our children away during all the years when they most needed us.

VIOLET, MARGERY AND AILEEN: MOTHER AND AUNTS

Violet aged twenty, in Burma

As well as the long reminiscences which I listened to in her last years, my mother left a pile of exercise books, diaries which started in her thirteenth year. They open when she was at her first and only school, the Ladies College in Eastbourne. She returned each term with an "Ugh" at the top of the page, but enjoyed the friendships and the learning, less the punishments. A popular one was to send her up to bed early, where in the dark cold dormitory she fell on her knees and stayed there until the other girls came up, pretty sure that the horrors that lurked behind the curtains would not dare to pounce on her in prayer.

God wasn't always protective though. She describes a thunder storm as "God's voice" sure that He was choosing June 1st 1909 to speak directly to her at Eastbourne Ladies College. This was the God of the Joneses, ever watchful, omnipresent, judging, punishing. Luckily he had a son who was gentle and often to be encountered by my mother in London fogs.

After a year of school her education was over, and her mother Annie came home to collect her elder sister Margery. Margery was an extremely clever girl who would have liked a career as a schoolmistress or missionary, but of course was not consulted. By the time Violet was ready to join the family in Burma, she would be safely married off. When Annie came home the three of them didn't live either at Drayton Gardens or with Beatrice in her luxury flat. Why not one wonders. This supposedly close and loving family often chose unlikely living arrangements.

The diary of 1914 opens when Violet, aged seventeen, is boarding with a family called James, and attending a Studio daily. Probably there was nothing much to say about the earlier years, even for an inventive Violet, but now life was going to begin at last. The Studio arranged for her to get a place at the Academy Schools, another spare aunt, her father's sister Alice was laid on as chaperone, and at 3, Templeton Place Violet started what she later described as the happiest year of her life.

Alice being a Swinhoe kept her temper, though she did occasionally irritate her headstrong niece by over chaperoning her. Alice later, when she was fifty five, had to go out and find herself a job, not ladylike but the only way she could survive since the remittances from Burma were often overlooked. She died in cheap rooms, occasioning a letter from Annie which began with the memorable words "The King dead, Kipling dead, and Aunt Alice terribly terribly ill". Annie wrote the letter with the body cooling off on the sofa, her real concern being that all Alice's rings were missing. They blamed the landlady, though it is more likely this nearly destitute spinster had had to flog them.

At eighteen Violet at last put her boring childhood behind her. She loved the work (she was talented) and the friendships, and she very soon became engaged to the star pupil, winner of the Gold Medal. The year started uncomfortably though when she got measles and was in an isolation hospital, very ill but still able to get a crush on her doctor. Harold Williamson prowled round with yellow roses, and soon afterwards they became engaged, but when the news reached the ears of the family there were snags. Harold was from the North (always suspect) and though not exactly working class, not in the full sense of the Jones word a gentleman. He had been to a Grammar School, his parents both worked and they kept only one servant. And they lived in Golders Green of all unmentionable places. There were interviews and letters to Burma.

All this was troublesome, but even more so Violet's mood swings. Everything he said seemed to send her off into sulks and tantrums. When he wrote of his love for classical music she accused him of belittling her, who preferred Gilbert and Sullivan. "I only said what I honestly meant or rather passionately felt" he soothed, "Dear Violet, naturally you and my ideals are intimately bound up. I can't separate you from my ideals and so I long for a home not only for you but where all the things I hate would not be and the things I love so much would and that is why your mention of this matter of music has touched me to the quick, though you may not understand." She didn't understand and with the pressures from the family the engagement was broken off. But then they made up, chose a "dinky little ring" and sat on a bench in the park feeling happy again. Violet's last entry for 1915 was "O my Beloved what will another year bring?"

It brought what she had secretly been hoping for, Harold's joining up. She said she found it embarrassing to be with a young man in a suit, though she never went as far as handing out white feathers. Harold's supposedly weak heart was overlooked as the need for cannon fodder grew, and he joined up as a private soldier. Violet was delighted at his departure for a freezing hut in Dorset to do his training, using his clever artist's hands to polish boots and learn how to shoot.

His first letters tell of how unpleasant it was to mix with the working classes. "Everything is very coarse, you go on eating pudding with your meat knife and fork. There is no one of my class really to associate with." Violet may have sympathised with this but didn't care to hear his moans about the dark, damp huts, the diet of tea, white bread and butter, stewed meat and carrots. She wasn't particularly interested in his regimen of carrying bales of marmalade up slippery hills either. With a tiny trace of irony he told her "You know my dear it is also very trying for me to know you have to submit to people and relations of various sorts, Aunt Alice for instance." At nineteen Violet had some justification for fretting under strict supervision, but her trials were hardly what Harold wanted to hear.

He was incensed by the treatment he and his fellows received., "the vast gulf between him and an OFFICER is so constantly being suggested by both soldiers and outsiders that already I am most nervous and ill at ease at going into any decent places. When I went to tea for instance the manageress immediately warningly gave me the price of what I wanted to have. People seem to have a general idea that nothing is too coarse for Tommies. You feel that in the Canteen too, where pianos with 4 notes abound, and illustrated papers a few years old."

Then he got measles. Spotty and segregated he got little comfort from Violet who had taken offence at something he said when on a brief leave. "My dear I never accused you of flirting" he assured her. "As to my unfortunate relations I can say that they are eminently reasonable and simple hearted people and feel sure you will like them more...I never intentionally cast a slur on your family not earning their living...it is more likely that your family would look down on ours because we earn ours. Having said a word in poor Mother's favour what is a poor man to do?" There wasn't much, and a letter he wrote after another brief meeting expresses what I also felt about Violet.

"Will you quietly teach me, Violet darling, how to understand you better so that when the part of you that terrifies me is foremost I can wait in patience and confidence for your dear loveable self to return? You see I could understand things like passionate outbursts of anger and so on, which one is used to in many people, but to be terrified of part of someone's character is a very new and strange experience for me. Should I take it that you have not only the usual essential feminine "moods" but have them in a phenomenal degree? I only want to be more philosophical in confidence that the real parts of your character are the ones I love...the only difficulty is that the lightning flashes are so vivid that at the time they strike me to the heart and make me think until they have gone "this is the blazing hateful reality".

After these less than restful leaves, he returned to the sordid business of being taught how to kill. His views became dangerous. "You know I have come to the conclusion that there is a lot of Prussianism in the British Army and after the war when the Kaiser and his satellites are hung, if you hung a great percentage of British officers millions of Englishmen would rejoice. It is being treated as scum that make the soldiers hate the army and it seems very serious to me that there should be such a bad spirit." Violet would have kept such scandalous outpourings to herself. It was a busy summer for her, she had met another man and was preparing to join her family in Burma. Once or twice the war really impinged though, as when on Tuesday May 5th "Pridham brought news of Lord Kitchener being drowned, what next I wonder?" she asked her diary. Next day she thought more deeply. "How terrible about Kitchener, I must go on the land and do my bit."

She came a little closer to the war itself on her summer trip to Deal. She found "very thrilling" the sight of shrapnel bursting from battles across the channel. On April 25th "After dinner I brushed Medora's hair, then crash boom ad lib. Zeppelins. Dashed up and fetched baby, turned out lights, put on hats and coats and gathered jewels. Went into the garden and heard its engines passing overhead, then saw flash of bombs dropping and it gradually passed away. Most thrilling and late to bed." The next night there was another raid during which "the nuns were chanting prayers, and Aunt Coco thumping gong for baby and Medora playing the piano" presumably making as much noise as possible to hide the sound of dropping bombs, though I can't place the nuns.

Although he didn't know about the new man in her life, Harold realised it was all over between them. "Had little box of flowers from Harold and heart rending little epitaph inside" Violet wrote, and then on August 2nd "H. left for France." On September 26th she noted "letter from Harold, he was wounded on the 15th and was in hospital in Salop." In spite of this casual comment, she kept his long letter about his experiences in the war, his crawling along the Crucifix trench in Delville wood and the death of his best friend. Harold went on to have two happy marriages and a successful career, ending up as principal of Chelsea College of Art. Why my mother kept his letters all those years in Burma and India I don't know. I finally returned them to his son.

Arnold Lambert had been in France for two years when Violet met him at a party in February 1916. For the next two years he wrote to her about once a month, mostly to Burma after her departure in September of that year. Back in France after their first meeting he addressed her "Dear Miss Swinhoe" and told her of his life in the trenches, leaving out the bad bits. "Our work is mostly done at night so that we sleep during most of the day, have breakfast at twelve noon and lunch at 5 p.m. and dinner at 3.a.m. Consequently we never know what day of the week it is or the date."

He had just read an English paper and was wry about the waffle of visiting journalists. "The soft snow flakes of purest white fell on stark bodies shrouding them tenderly. It was as if the doves of peace were flying to fold their wings over the obscene scenes of war...the guns were silent, there was no sniping as the scurrying flakes put a veil between the trenches" The snow certainly put a veil between the trenches, said Arnold, but that made it necessary to keep the guns going to prevent an attack under cover of the blizzard.

He told her of the reality of snow. "Two days ago it was snowing and a bitter east wind blowing...We are not fond of wind with east in it as it is then favourable for Hun gas attacks." One evening a thrush sang above the barking of the guns but "the finer the weather the livelier the opposing artilleries so that just when one wants to stroll out into the fields and back in the sun one is vividly and suddenly reminded there is a war on and one has to scuttle for cover like a young rabbit."

On June 31st he had time and energy to write at some length. "I stood on a ridge this evening as the sun was setting and gazed across a huge expanse of country, becoming less and less distinct as the evening mists thickened in the valley and crept up the sides of the hill. In that band of gathering mist I could see a long line of upturned chalk disappearing into the distance north and south - the firing line...For fully fifteen minutes not a rifle or gun fired. It was easy to imagine that after all the war was an infernal dream and that really people were quite sane and civilised. But as soon as the darkness became more tangible the usual display of starshells commenced between the two lines, repeated bursts of machine fire rent the heavy air and echoed and re-echoed over the rows of battered houses. As the darkness deepens also, the evacuation of wounded starts, and those who can walk step out over the open if it is sufficiently quiet and make what speed they can to the nearest ambulance. They are wonderfully cheery too. But now I must be boring you."

By November 25th when she had left for Burma he addressed her as Dearest Chubbie and thanked her for the present of a woolly waistcoat sent from Port Said. At the risk of boring her again he said, he told her "I am at Forward Billets surrounded by guns of all shapes and sizes. The larger ones when they fire put all the lights out in our hut and make everything dance off the shelves and table - result outer darkness and inner wrath, confusion and "langwidge". The surrounding ground is one honeycomb of shell holes varying from one foot in depth to twenty. It is raining, it is night, it is intensely dark, it is exceedingly muddy, it is - unmentionable."

He told her of an "adventure" which I think won for him his Military Cross. "I had an exciting job three days ago. There is a very old Abbey near the front line which was recently captured from the Bosches. They had made extensive use of its vaults as dugouts, consequently they kept up an almost continuous barrage of shellfire on and around it. A report came that there were underground passages from it to a village in the lines. My proper job was not 500 yards from the Abbey, so watching my opportunity I dashed across when there was a lull and finding a hole in the huge pile of brick debris I retired from the outer world somewhat precipitately into the yawning black pit beneath. I found myself, after a few moments, on a pile of bricks which came clattering after me in one of the vaults. From this vantage point I could be quite rude to the shells bursting above. My orderly, temporarily amazed at my disappearance gazed from above with such a look of wonderment I burst into fits of laughter. However I found another entrance of less steep descent and got him in.

We then explored all the vaults which were full of German coats, helmets, arms and equipment, and finally found the entrance under the vaults to the underground passages. These were hewn out of the solid chalk some fifty feet below ground. They were so small in places that we had to crawl on our tummies. This was not easy holding a revolver in one hand and a candle in the other and when the candle went out - what darkness, stillness, utter isolation from the world. Unfortunately none of the passages went very far before they were blocked up. I made a rough survey of the whole place and when we finally emerged it was dark with thick mist and as we were carrying a heavy box away between us (a German trench mortar) we fell every three yards over roots of trees, shell holes, barbed wire etc. And didn't we simply overboil with heat...I made the others in the Mess green with envy, with a hair raising account of it at dinner. Except one who had to go next day and dig a trench into the vaults."

That January was exceedingly cold. "The hut we sleep in is made of a light wood frame and covered with tarred felt, which of course is not very good stuff for keeping a keen north wind out. So cold it is in the morning that our sponges, soap, towels and boots are absolutely stiff and just where our noses peep out of the blankets the condensation from our breath freezes in a little cake on them." In May he became a Captain and was entitled to a second horse. "She is such a ripping, graceful, slender little dear with legs of exquisite shape and feet - well a wee bit small if anything - I can't think why I call her Bobbina" (his pet name for Violet).

Though they had met only two or three times, their separation and his exciting times drew them together. "Oh Bobbina mea, why are you so far away, or perhaps why am I?" he sighed. "If the fates were a little less cruel and I could see you just occasionally I might suggest very carefully at first and then a wee bit more plainly an "idea" which has been germinating within me, an idea which grows daily more insistent in spite of the fact that my inner self realises its hopelessness. " Another year was to pass before he sent her a ring, which arrived not long before her wedding day, July 10th 1918. Arnold survived the shells, but got flu after the Armistice which turned to pneumonia after a terrible journey in an unheated train. His sister wrote to Violet that she had begged to be allowed to nurse him in the field hospital in France where he was lying but was refused permission. After his death on Christmas Day his family simply got his medal and a curt note.

In his last letter to her Arnold wrote; "Violet please write and tell me that all my fears are groundless and that the promise you made to at least wait till the end of the war is not going to be too difficult to keep...My dugout is swarming with mice and a few rats but as it is extremely late I must risk having this letter devoured during the night." Their time together had been so short that it was too much to hope that Violet, in the sweet seductive airs of Mandalay, would keep her head and heart steady. In fact she got engaged several times in the rather over enthusiastic way she had with men.

After she died at the age of ninety, I read a few pages of the last diary she kept almost to the end. At the top of the page for May 29th she had written in capital letters "My great and special day" and I puzzled over this until I read the earlier diary of 1916, when she described the May day she and Arnold spent together, she in the sidecar of his motorbike as they rode out into the country; a shower of rain, a picnic with ginger beer, nettles; nothing special except that it shone out of her past with an intensity that left the rest of her life shadowed. Pinned to the pile of Arnold's letters in her drawer was a poem.

> "As a perfume doth remain
> In the folds where it hath lain
> So the thought of you remaining
> Deeply folded in my brain
> Will not leave me - all things leave me

You remain."

If she had married him, and settled down as the wife of an engineer in England, neither I nor my children would have had to follow the Old Trail out East. But of course we wouldn't have been us.

When my mother headed for Burma in September 1916 she was leaving behind her a rootless childhood. No more "blowings up" from Aunt Coco in Deal, no more agitated scoldings from Aunt Alice, no more "mooching about" in boarding houses, no more love conducted on park benches. The Burma she arrived in as she floated up river from Rangoon to Mandalay was a land of beautiful people, golden pagodas, infinite fun. Her diaries written up to her marriage eighteen months later are a catalogue of parties, picnics, and best of all rides along the river banks. She spoke of "queering the pitch" of her sister Margery, who very soon got herself engaged and married, to the great regret of everybody, including herself.

It was on Friday August 17th in the hill station Maymyo that Violet first mentioned my father. "Lemons and Captain James to dinner, had to drag the last by force." Five days later they were playing golf together, and on September 1st at a dance "had two with James and he was ripping and there was a full moon and altogether everything was top hole." But it was not exactly a whirlwind romance. In her diaries he is "old James" or "our James" and on December 12th she went to the races and "behold old Sleepy James". By the following March he was still writing to her as Miss Swinhoe but on March 19th " Began dancing and was at the 4th when he told me he loved me. Dear thing, but I said I was so uncertain in my mind...Told mother and she thought and D. too that he was a bit quiet." However he was thirty two, white, steady and solvent, so they soon got over their misgivings. She continued to have quite a lot.

On March 30th "Will had final talk with Daddy and then we were engaged. Too queer for words. I lay down." With the arrival of Arnold's ring there was a flutter in the family and the wedding was postponed and Will, rousing himself from his sleepiness, talked of "breaking it off". He got malaria, Violet wept quite a lot, but they arrived at the altar on July 10th in Maymyo. My mother could never clearly explain what Will was doing in Burma as a political officer. He had been wounded in Mesopotamia which explained his absence from the battle front, and somewhere along the way had learnt Yunnanese she said. Strangely I never talked to him about his life before he entered the Jones's.

So she had arrived at her inevitable destination, the altar, towards which everything in her life had been directed. Her talents had been fostered for just this moment, her prettiness rejoiced over, her social graces groomed so that a man would take her off her parents' hands for the rest of her life. She did not reflect that by marrying in the East her own children would suffer the same fate she had done, father a remote unknown figure, mother returning at intervals in order to negotiate the next transfer to the next unwilling aunt. My mother's largely unloved childhood, largely unschooled as well though she was exceptionally clever, affected her in ways a daughter can only guess at. I think it made her restless, always in search of the Good Times she had so signally missed. It made her brave and resourceful, able to transform drab reality into romantic drama. It made her manipulative, since she had spent a childhood outwitting the Joneses, ducking from their sudden rages, skipping aside from the "scenes". Lying must have been second nature then, and continued to be.

Tipped out of their bullock cart into the sand on their honeymoon, she and Will dusted themselves down and plodded on till they found another. Dusting and plodding their way through a long marriage, they remained fond and forgiving. Which is more than can be said for Margery and her husband whose tormented life together started before Violet's and Will's and whose children were a pair of disasters waiting to happen.

Violet and Will's wedding, 1918

My aunt Margery

Margery was my mother's older sister. Like Violet, she spent her early years with the Roberts family in Blackheath, and then got a good education at Eastbourne Ladies College, the money not having run out as it did for Violet. She loved its chill disciplined airs, and the total absence of men, and would like to have continued the same sort of life as a schoolmistress or missionary. She was very beautiful, with the wide brow and deep set eyes of her mother, but from her earliest photographs she scowls. In Violet's diaries she "flares up" and is "ratty" almost every day. Her difficult moods did not deter her parents from handing her over to a Captain Roy Lemon. Later he accused the family of hiding insane skeletons in their cupboards. He handed his own deeply disturbed daughter over to a bridegroom with the same skilful deception though.

Rodway and Annie, her parents, in their eagerness to settle Margery, overlooked the fact that her husband was a Jew. Later when things went wrong this "tainted" strain was blamed, since both Swinhoes and Joneses were heavily anti semitic. Everybody wept a lot at Margery's wedding, and when she returned from her honeymoon she confided to Violet that "it" was horrible, but she was soon pregnant. This daughter Sheila was followed five years later by a son Leigh, and a governess was brought out to Burma for them. My mother said the son, the Chota Sahib (young lord) was spoilt and pampered and Sheila, dark and Jewish looking (horrors) was neglected.

They were taken home when Sheila was ten, and trouble followed fast and furious. Spoilt Leigh couldn't settle into the discipline of Prep and Public schools. I forget how many schools he went to and how many actually expelled him and for what reasons. The war came as a relief to the family as it took him off into the Air force where he was able to use his considerable engineering skills. But civvy street when he returned to it was boring, and he livened things up by climbing onto the roof of an Oxford college, creeping in at the windows and stealing sheets which he flogged on the black market. He was gaoled for six months, the shame of which meant that Margery had to leave Oxford, where the family were living, and go and live in Devon. He became involved with various women, married two of them and after the second divorce left the country after refusing to pay alimony. There he married a German with whom he settled down happily, out of the reach of his mother. This happy ending was denied Sheila, whose life was fairly steadily disastrous to the end.

Why she had a nervous breakdown at fourteen isn't clear. It was of course her mother's manic behaviour that triggered off her collapse. I was spending holidays with Aunt Margery at that time, and remember a morning when Sheila came down to breakfast in a blue velvet dress, which I thought very impressive. Margery, at the sight of her, went into one of her uncontrollable rages, screaming that she looked like a Whitechapel Jew, hitting her about the head and ordering

98

her upstairs for the rest of the day. Meals with Margery were especially dangerous. "Smug little beast" she would yell at one or other of us, and knives would fly. The very smell of her house; disinfectant, galoshes, boiling cabbage; was full of menace.

One day Sheila picked up a knife herself. I remember the scene, the scuffling and shrieks, and though no damage was done Sheila was removed to Rampton and stayed there for two years, in a padded cell my mother said. It was only when Margery went to India for a brief while that Lawrence had her released. What to do with her? Send her East of course, and marry her to anyone available, without telling him she had been in a lunatic asylum. At first all seemed to go well in her marriage, but after the birth of a son rumours of "rows" began to circulate. The marriage was due to be dissolved, but before this happened Sheila went off into the woods and took an overdose of sleeping pills. Margery and my mother were always convinced it was murder and continued to say so for years, though nobody listened.

Margery, the real killer in a roundabout way, lived on in Exmouth with a clear conscience. She looked after her mother Annie until she died at the age of ninety-three, the news of this death conveyed to Violet on a postcard. Four months later she covered four sheets of paper describing the death of her labrador dog and the infinite distress this caused her. After the postcard a letter to Violet poured out her bitterness. "I looked after Mother for fifteen years, buying all her clothes, even a fur coat, and poor Roy got heartily sick of it when we were so hard up every penny counted, but when we asked you to have her while we visited our first grandchild you couldn't keep her more than ten days because when you searched through her papers you discovered she had not cash to give you so you told us we must come and fetch her. After her death you came down with 2 large empty suitcases and returned home laden. So all along the line I must have no reward for years of patient care and give in to every claim from you."

It was one of the curiosities of my mother, that she kept all the really nasty letters people wrote her, which anyone else would have torn up into little pieces and stamped on. Here was a typical Jones, raking up old grievances, wildly exaggerating (Annie had quite a comfortable income from shares, and Roy a Brigadier's pension), the spiteful prods, the general unforgivingness. After all the tragedies of her life Margery was the same erratic, explosive person, ready to fly off whatever handle presented itself. After Roy's death she moved to a smaller house. "It may take some time to sell this house" she wrote to Violet "but I am starting to use up this notepaper in faith. We have such a wonderful Saviour." Deeply religious to the end, she damaged everyone she came into contact with, but continued on her destructive way without a twinge of regret. She salved whatever conscience she had by leaving most of her money and possessions to the church.

Poor Aunt Aileen

The third of this generation of Jones girls who went East was Aileen. I tell her story because in some curious ways, particularly in her madness, it reverberates with my experience. Aileen was my grand-mother Annie's sister Beatrice's daughter. Aileen was born in Buenos Aires, fathered by the best-forgotten Fred. She spent a luxurious childhood, never travelling further than Kent, and then with nurses and governesses. Then when she was eighteen, pretty, pampered and vulnerable, her mother handed her over to a middle-aged tea planter Hugh Swinhoe, a cousin, younger brother of the inefficient sweet maker Docie. Home on leave from Assam he proposed first to Beatrice, who was still handsome and rich, but reluctant to leave her London life for the jungles of Assam, she offered him Aileen instead. Of all the Jones deals this was surely the most heartless. Aileen must have been a spiritless girl to put up no resistance. It could be she thought India an exotic destination.

My mother, who was at the wedding in September 1914 reported that Aileen looked placid but not ecstatic, and that Hugh was not <u>very</u> fat. In the only photograph I have of them a year later on the tea garden he is very fat indeed, a mountain of a man leaning over a woman with black smudges under her eyes. This was not surprising since she had been transported from Hyde Park Mansions to a steamy, malarial valley, remotely stationed between the Himalayas and the Naga Hills, home of head hunters. Tea thrived in the humidity, and so did snakes, mosquitoes and endless varieties of insects. White women, of whom there were few in 1914, noticeably did not. The resources Aileen took with her to this sweaty backwater were a neat way with a needle, a repertoire of tuneful ballads, and how to arrange cutlery and glassware on dinner tables. The sodden uncultured life of Assam found no use for such skills.

After a long sea journey, there was a four day train trip from Calcutta, and then a river steamer to cross the Brahmaputra. They finally drove over miles of bumpy roads to the tea garden, and the bungalow which was still standing when I went to Assam thirty years later. It was a large thatched building, prettily climbed over by flowering creepers. Its dark rooms opened onto a wide wooden verandah, green shrouded. Beyond the compound was the tea, dry and spiky when she first saw it in October. After Hyde Park Mansions what did she think of this dark, insect infested house? It was without electricity or sanitation, and miles from another white woman. How had Hugh ever imagined that Beatrice might like it? The insects especially appalled Aileen, who had only seen bumble bees and houseflies while here, outsize, they buzzed and crawled and bit day and night.

In this menacing menagerie, because there were also lizards and snakes and enormous bats and wild cats and tigers roaring in the jungle, Aileen sat alone most of the time, Hugh joining her for meals of roast goat or stringy little chickens. Company was rare and male, talk of tea, polo and shikar. There was no library, no music, no magazines, no shopping, no gossip, the staples of her normal life. Perhaps once a fortnight they would drive over dusty roads to the club, where she would watch polo or tennis, and then wait for the men to totter out of their private bar. On the way home they might see a wild elephant; Assam was a botanist's paradise, a zoologist's dream, but to a gently reared girl used to seeing animals clinically caged, it was a nightmare.

Her son would have been conceived when white simul cotton seed was blowing in clouds across the lawn, her morning sickness begun with the Persian Lilac spraying pale mauve petals on the grass. Thunder and lightning would crash and blaze over her in the monsoon, ants swarm in to drop their wings in the soup, snakes find refuge from the rain under the dining room table. My mother often referred to the Botched Birth of Basil, but in exactly what way it was botched I don't know. There were so many ways in Assam in 1915. Perhaps the doctor didn't arrive, or when he did he was drunk. It could be that the water, heated in kerosene tins, was not hot enough to kill germs. Puerperal fever was followed by post natal depression. Aileen couldn't be left alone with the baby. Hugh had to stay with her, and after some months of neglecting his work he was sacked. Within the year mother and child were home, Hugh found himself another post and the marriage was over.

She returned to her mother, at first to comfort and support. They lived in their grand house and forgot about Hugh who died a few years later leaving an estate of £150. Little Basil was handed over to nursemaids. He recalled that his mother went one day to see him bathed and was surprised that his legs were like sticks. She was told that at three years old he had hardly been taken out of his pram and could barely walk. All through his childhood he was pushed out of the way, sent to boarding schools and in the holidays to anyone who would have him. Perhaps he reminded his mother of the debacle of her marriage; of fat Hugh and the insects and the botched birth. But it was not a kind revenge.

In fact Aileen never really recovered from her breakdown in India. When her mother Beatrice died she soldiered on for a bit, but one day Basil returned to find she had smashed the place to pieces, and been taken off to a Home. Of course nobody had ever warned him that she might break down again at the menopause, or indeed that she had broken down before. My mother said that after that she simply disappeared to an unknown address where she died, presumably. Nobody was informed or cared. The whole story with its cruel cover ups and callous forgetfulness was typical of the time. Aileen, creamy complexion, rich mother and all had as few choices as anyone else. After all there was always the hope that she would have enjoyed the best of fates, Beatrice's delightful life as a wealthy widow.

Lined up in their photographs they look serene and beautiful these Jones women. They were comfortably off, adequately educated, with the looks and social skills to attract suitors. But for some the suitors never came and for some the wrong ones turned up, and since there was no real life outside marriage these had to be accepted and lived with till death did them part. The choice between an unhappy marriage or the stultifying tedium of spinsterhood and Staying with Mother was all that was on offer to the first generation of Juxon and Maria's family. Their blazing rows may have simply relieved the tedium. Violet, Margery and Aileen, the second generation, also knew that any other ambition than the altar was not for them. Even I, the third generation, confided to my diary the grim prospect of never getting a "proposal" and asked myself how I would survive the shame. There was always India though, the provider of husbands for girls and jobs for boys, our inevitable and face-saving destination.

IRIS: YOUTH

Iris aged about eight

My being a daughter was, to start with, the one really successful thing about my childhood: before I got polio, and was found to have missed out on the good looks of my parent's families. The word "daughter" when first pronounced by my parents was full of promise, of future pride. A pretty daughter would be such a credit to them. After my mother died I came across a family photograph proudly labelled "The Happy Family" in my mother's hand. She sat with her three sons (Monty was born three years after me) and the space where I should have been was blotted out. My sixty year old throat tightened, tears quite close, as I realised how early and how much my appearance mattered to my parents, and how disappointed they were.

It was on the boat going home from India at eight months old that I became "seedy" and my right leg "sort of shrivelled". Not a lot was made of this, strangely because Infantile Paralysis was a well known disease, often fatal. My mother had to go into hospital when we got home, but nobody suggested I should be examined. My birth had done something unpleasant to her insides and she was being "tidied up"; all her labours were dramatic, the source of a blood-filled ballad embellished over the years, the punch line being "And then the doctor said I was never to have another", advice often handed out to women of her generation with no instructions as to how this was to be achieved.

Back in India for four years it became apparent that my right leg was not going to fill out and was a couple of inches shorter than the other. The subject was never discussed in the family, my mother hated disfigurement of any kind, and it must have been a sore trial, perhaps even a "curse", that her only daughter was disabled. Treatment of polio meant leg irons even in bed, and a little later on surgical boots, but I was sure my leg would get better. This would happen when I was thirteen, an impossibly long time ahead but absolutely assured, in time to see me going even-legged into adolescence. I would take off my irons and watch the muscles return to my dropped foot. The rather unpleasant treatments; rubber bands buttoned round my calf and electric currents passed through, would end. I would no longer lie in dark glasses under ultra violet rays, nor be "manipulated" by a smart charlatan in Park Lane. A sort of drawbridge would be let down over which I would walk without a limp into a promising future.

There was one last interview with the Specialist in his large dim consulting room and my mother and I stepped glumly out into a London street, saying nothing, nothing was ever said. My Bad Leg was a taboo subject in the family, but she had consolations in her handsome sons, who were provided with tennis rackets, golf clubs, cricket bats, which I watched them play with, hiding my bad leg in its built up shoe behind my good one. Because entering my teens my life became dedicated to trying to hide it from the public gaze, to cross a room became an exercise in camouflage. Even in the hottest summers; and the summers of the thirties were very hot; I carried a coat over my right arm, to drape itself down my side and conceal my leg. Neither my mother nor my aunts thought of giving me slacks to wear. I dreamt and schemed of buying myself a pair, but in the days before dress allowances this was impossible. Why did I never ask? I don't know, the young were so tongue tied then, adults so crushingly in control.

My pet name in the family was Jane, short for Plain Jane, so by the time I was educated and ready to be taken to India to find a husband, my chances were considered to be poor, especially by me. A third crippling disadvantage was a good brain. Men hated clever women my mother never ceased to point out, and even quite old very clever men in the Indian Civil Service would prefer not to have the silence in their remote outposts disturbed by intelligent conversation. Nevertheless their presence as potential husbands for me cheered us all.

Looking back, my polio could be considered as one of the great character forming experiences of my life, like being sent to boarding school at six, and living with my Aunt Margery. Our journey back from India for the second time was to put my brothers and I into schools, and it was enlivened by running out of money half way home. This disembarking in Italy on Christmas Eve became one of my mother's best stories. She said she had been sending regular sums of money to Thomas Cook's, and their agent was supposed to be waiting with it at Bordigera, so as to pay our passage on. He never appeared, so a bedraggled little family turned up at a boarding house where the kind landlady not only took us in but provided us with bags of nuts as presents. Like a lot of my mother's stories this took some believing, but what could have been a disaster turned into an interesting holiday. The boys were sent to school, and my parents joined the local ex pats in outings. When we eventually got home to Sidmouth photographs show us in woollen bathing suits drooping round our calves, our hair blowing in the sea wind, which makes one wonder why they ever left Italy.

My father returned to India and I saw him only twice more during my childhood, a stranger for whom my feelings were neutral. My mother stayed at home and rented a house in Berkhamstead. It was very small but we had a Cook General and her daughter as a Daily. The cook was called Mrs Carver, appropriately as she was a quick tempered lady who hurled bone handled carving knives at her daughter when annoyed. Bank statements of the time show my mother to have been overdrawn by £200, a tidy sum, but she talked in her letters about getting a live in governess. The kind of poverty we were always being reminded of, that kept pocket money to the minimum and meant wearing school uniforms in the holidays, never envisaged anything so drastic as doing without servants.

I went to my first school in Berkamstead, and a letter written by my mother sent the comforting assurance to my father that he needn't worry about my education. She had been told by my headmistress that I was the brightest child she had ever had under her roof; a small one admittedly. Instead of pondering

105

how to best train their little prodigy they heaved sighs of relief that she would need only a passing pat on the head as she went on her clever little way. In fact it became their ultimate care to damp down my fires of intellect and to steer me away from becoming a "blue stocking". I was sixty before my mother told me that my last school had been confident that I would get a scholarship to Oxford, but she had taken me out to India instead.

Berkhamstead is a blur from which emerge sharp pictures; of Mrs Carver's cutlery flying past my nose; of getting lost on the way back from school and panicking amongst gigantic strangers; of sitting on the doorstep shelling peas and suddenly remembering I should have gone to tea with Andrew and feeling shock that stays with me still, why I can't imagine. There was ecstasy too when my mother brought home a tortoise, and agony when it disappeared. There was no sense that this was the beginning of the end, that the family was about to break into pieces and never reassemble again.

When my mother went back to India my brothers went as boarders to Berkhamstead School, and I to a school in Watford. I was six, and I remember on the first evening sitting by the window of the Common Room with the laurels in the rain outside tapping against the glass, night and aloneness of a kind so desolating that all other separations take me back to it; coldness against my cheek, and the night wind shaking the wetness from the leaves in the huge blackness of the world. I remember the tune that was running through my head; "Massas in the cold, cold ground". I still hum it in times of trouble.

I think I was the youngest pupil in the school, and so always the one accused of making smells. We would stand in a row in front of the Common Room table and a bigger girl, perhaps eight, would sniff our behinds, finding mine the one to blame. I would be banished to the lavatory, locked in until they thought fit to release me. I never got within yards of the thick grey radiators, and was also young enough to be taken in by stories of the instruments of torture kept by the headmistress in her room. Thumb screws and lighted tapers up your nails were the very least you could expect if ever summoned to her presence. There were some offences so terrible that she kept earwigs ready to put into one ear, so that they could chomp their way through your brain to get out the other.

One of these heinous sins was to use the front staircase, which led to the hall outside the headmistress's study. A delicious shiver of fear shook us as we stood at the top of the stairs and dared one another to run down them. Luckily I had found out about Jesus and prayed every night Never Never I Beg of Thee allow anyone to push me down the Staircase. As often happened He chose to ignore my pleas, and there came a day when the other girls had been chasing me with frightful threats, and my only escape was down the Staircase. I stood trembling at the top, weighing up the terrifying alternatives, stroking the glossy wood which slithered under my damp palms. Behind me were my tormentors, at the bottom of the stairs Miss Norris waiting like a spider outside her front door, to drag me into her web and torture me. In the end I went down, jelly slithering from a spoon. No Miss Norris, but when I got back to the Common Room the inquisition.

How had I got back without being seen? Had I gone down the Staircase? Had I? Had I? I'll start at the beginning I said, but they didn't want that, they wanted me to confess so that they could Report me. And then the bell rang for chapel. I used every second of the time on my knees making pacts with Jesus; my whole entire life was offered in lieu of a lapse of memory on the part of my persecutors. And this time He listened. Not another word was said about the stairs. It was a miracle, and the next six years were spent reasonably dedicated to His service in the ways that were available to me, praying a lot on hard floors and giving up sugar for Lent.

One other memory returns very clearly from the Watford school. I was out on the playing fields jumping up and down while the others practised shooting at netball. Like a dog waiting for a stick, I hoped for a ball to be thrown my way. Suddenly I saw Matron plodding across the field towards us. I can see her still as a matter of fact, stiff and upright with her starched cap blowing in the breeze. With a solemn face she told me that the headmistress wished to see me, and led me away. No prisoner on the way to the gallows could have felt more terrified. Miss Norris only saw you for torture or Being Expelled. Matron took me into her room wordlessly, and left me standing in front of her desk. She was resting her beige woollen bosom on the blotting paper in front of her, and beckoned me forward. I was so stiff with terror I couldn't even turn round to look for thumb screws. She had a letter on the desk, and told me it was from my mother. My little brother in India had been very ill, so ill in fact that in the end he hadn't been able to live. I still remember that she couldn't use the word "died", but the news in whatever guise came to me as an excruciating relief.

There was a puzzled look on Miss Norris's face, not expecting the broad grin that greeted her news. Now there were to be no lighted tapers beneath my nails, no earwigs plodding across my brain. Back at the netball post I told the girls that my brother had died and they crowded round patting my back and saying "Rotten luck" and "Gosh you're being brave". For several days they allowed me near the radiator and offered acid drops. I wondered if there were any other relations who could give their lives to prolong this lovely amnesty. I hardly remembered Monty and didn't have the imagination to feel my parents' pain, forgivable but looking back a bit insensitive.

In the holidays my brothers and I went to the Vicarage at Potten End, which was run as a Home for children of the Raj, one of many at the time. The Vicar seemed very old to me, and had a long beard which spent most of its time resting on the sheet in front of him, dusted with crumbs; he always appears in my memory in bed in a room that was dark and full of the smells of stale urine and medicines. I can't remember his wife, but he had a daughter called Kitty, who once did a handstand at the bottom of the bed, revealing knickers stained with blood. It is a curious memory; the sick Vicar, Kitty's stout legs swaying in the yellowish air to amuse a six year old, who was not amused and too shy to point out to Kitty that she had cut herself.

We roamed the Vicarage grounds, the boys and girls whose parents were Abroad, and the moor behind which was threaded with little paths which I made into the roads of a private kingdom. This I shared with Jesus and a collection of animals, whose daily job it was to bring back into bracken dens fruit cake and thick slices of suet pudding. Jesus in his white nightdress and the tigers and bears and green-eyed wolves sat in the bracken and ate imaginary meals to try to fill the gap left by the sparse Vicarage fare. The bitter smell of bracken still brings back hunger and a circle of animals crouched round Jesus and I.

Once we went on an outing with the Women's Institute to Hampton Court. We went in a charabanc carrying cucumber sandwiches; oh the bliss of a stomach absolutely filled with soggy bread; the slimy filling I put in my blazer pocket and dropped into the flower beds when we arrived. When I wasn't on the moor I spent a lot of time planning how not to be seen going in and out of the lavatory, which was a shed in the garden. The shame of being spotted using this was not to be borne, so I scouted round the bushes and dived in when the coast was clear. Coming out was more difficult, and meant standing on the seat and peering out, and even then there was always the risk of bumping into the gardener and blushing to my guilty ears with embarrassment. When my young friends worry whether they can leave their six year olds for a weekend with Granny, I am reminded of that small figure tiptoe on the lavatory seat full of an unshareable panic.

Monty's death brought my mother home a year early, and we were at the Vicarage when she arrived. She must have been heartbroken, but showed us no sign of it, courage of a kind that was typical of her. She rented a house in Littlehampton and I thought this was to be home. Cousins came in the summer to play with us on the beach, and go for cycle rides on the downs. I went to a new school and to reach it crossed an enchanted fairy-filled wood. Years later I went back and found it was a traffic island. When she returned to India I was left as a boarder at the school, and at eight years old started the era of unknown holidays; to aunts, to a farm in Suffolk and when my prayers were answered to my grandmother. The Vicarage put the lid on Holiday Homes, my mother had found us half starved there.

Real life took place at school, which was called Furzedown and was run on P.N.E.U. lines with a brilliant if eccentric headmistress who taught me nearly everything I ever learnt. Nothing could have been less like Miss Norris than the artistic, emotional and exotically pious Miss Fidler. She was an inspired teacher, which was just as well since she taught us everything except Maths and Netball, for which a Miss Thom was brought in whose bulbous calves are the only thing I remember about her. There was a gentle music teacher too who took us for Eurythmics when we dressed in green silk tunics and stretched our arms up to the sun pretending to be daffodils or fields of corn.

Miss Fidler was the maypole round which the whole school danced. During lessons our aim was to be called to her side, her arm around us, and then if we were lucky slid onto her lap for full Petting. Petting settled your status, how many times, for how long was discussed and gloated over. In the afternoons we went for walks in crocodiles along the promenade, dressed in mud brown coats and in winter woollen caps to match, in the summer straw hats in the shape of Salvation Army bonnets. Neither did much for my pasty face, lidless eyes, putty nose as photos of the time show. I was unaware of my looks, nor bothered about the boots I had to wear. I couldn't understand why I wasn't chosen to play the Angel Gabriel in the Nativity Play in my last year, the plum part which was given to a girl three years younger with long yellow hair and big blue eyes.

Half way through our walks Miss Fidler's voice would rise above the sea wind to cry "Break crocodile" and all of us would turn and hurl ourselves at her, like rugby players in front of the goal. A fortunate pair got hold of her hands, and was allowed to hold them until we turned for home. I can still feel the squared stones of the esplanade beneath my boots, the gritty wind in my face, and the blessed leathery warmth of Miss Fidler's fur gloved hand enclosing mine. I had a fur glove fetish for years.

Her hold over us, sickly as it now seems, was part of her excellence as a teacher. She literally held us spellbound when she read poetry to us, or took us into the past, or led us into the countryside and showed us wild flowers. Crafts were an important part of P.N.E.U. teaching, and we sawed plywood and dented pewter to please her, my fretsaw ploughing its way through my desk in my frantic desire to finish a toast rack for her. She wasn't pleased, but her displeasure could lead to forgiveness and a possible Petting. We wove miles of raffia round bits of cardboard and squeezed damp clay into the shapes of dogs and cats, indistinguishable from each other, and cut potatoes up to colour and stamp out onto the covers of albums to give her as presents. Later, when I taught my own children on P.N.E.U lines, these skills became useful at last.

It was all heady stuff, but the best part of all was Miss Fidler's devotion to the Vicar, the very High Church Father Orr. It was his Highness that eventually had me removed from the school, but for the couple of years before the terrible truth was discovered I revelled in incense and candles and Confession once a week, when Father Orr, who was about ten feet tall, laid his violet-scented hands on my head and forgave me the sins I had spent the previous six days saving up for him. Confession was made easier for us by little red books listing all the sins it was possible to commit, which we ticked our way through, putting a question mark by adultery. We made our bedside lockers into chapels, with matchbox altars bearing tiny silver paper chalices. On the bottom shelf of the locker we kept caterpillars in cardboard boxes, so that our chapels smelt of dead leaves and droppings but this didn't seem to spoil our chanting devotions after Lights Out.

Jesus was no longer the barefooted white robed figure of the moorland picnics. He was not unlike Father Orr, tall, sweet smelling and demanding. We brought home thistles to flagellate ourselves, and laid us down on the lino flooring to sleep, hoping to curry favour with Him since we couldn't get hold of any hair shirts. If any awful crime was committed, such as leaving dirty finger marks on the roller towels in the bathroom, we Owned Up en masse and endured the punishment of eating porridge without sugar or milk, forcing the gluey lumps down in the glow of martyrdom.

The only fly in this rich ointment was Matron, she of the stockinged feet who prowled the corridors at night to catch us at some unlawful activity; she of the morning lavatory patrol whose sharp judgment "That's not enough, go back and try again" forced me into collecting bits of wood and floating them in the lavatory bowl, half concealed with toilet paper. Matrons now seem to me a sad species, women down on their luck, widows with a pittance on which to rear families, who went their thankless rounds in schools, stacking sheets and smelling vests to see if we had changed them after games. This one had a freckled son called Dampier who went to Christ's Hospital and spent his holidays with her in the school. His appearance in his navy and scarlet robes had us in a flutter of excitement which we thought might be adultery.

Leaving all this for holidays with Aunt Evelyn in her freezing villa on top of a one-in-four incline, or Aunt Hilda in her house backing onto a railway line, was an anti-climax. These aunts were my father's sisters, who had left their husbands in India, and settled with their children at home. My mother thought this a very selfish choice, but made good use of them all the same. I never thought about it at the time, nor questioned why my cousins had permanent homes and we didn't. The choices made by adults were outside my frame of reference until a great deal later.

Aunt Evelyn, like the Vicar, spent a lot of her time in bed it seemed to me, with a disease that gave her yellow fingers and hair. In fact she was a chain smoker, and bed was probably the only warm place in her arctic house. I slept with various cousins in the attic, warmed through the round holes of a paraffin stove. I had chilblains all my childhood on my bad leg, from ankle to thigh. As I forced my throbbing nail scratched leg into my surgical boot I asked Jesus if he couldn't bring forward my cure, make it eleven instead of thirteen. No luck though.

Aunt Evelyn didn't really need to get out of bed to organise us, because our routine was fixed and unchanging; mornings playing on a deserted tennis court, afternoons going for walks down a Roman road, a wintry road in my memory, ice when there wasn't mud. There were occasional excitements, like the feud we had with the family next door who we called the Miller Monkeys. One long afternoon I spent with my hair tied to a hedge by these enemies, unable to get free, until my cries were heard by "our side". I must have been too paralysed with fear to loosen the knot or pull out some strands of hair. In the evenings we played card games, and last thing at night Aunt Evelyn climbed up into the attic to kiss us good night. This simple and kindly act terrified me. I was convinced her yellow fingers were going to grip me round the throat. This changing of a familiar figure into a monster has always seemed the most terrifying prospect, the stuff of horror stories. I expect it was at this age the theme of many of the fairy tales I was reading.

Holidays with Aunt Hilda were spent in a shed, rehearsing for a performance we spent every waking moment preparing for. My cousins went to ballet school, but with my booted leg my part consisted of holding a parasol over their heads as they pirouetted on their stuffed pink shoes. How long the years till thirteen seemed, until I too could put my strong foot into a satin shoe and tie laces round a sturdy calf. I read a lot of books on ballet so that I could be ready, and positively pestered Jesus. One of my cousins, Barbara, nearly died of a mastoid operation one holiday, and with her ears stuffed with cotton wool shared my peripheral status. She was impressed with my holiness, and the pair of us made a pact that we would try to get ourselves crucified in return for what Jesus had done for us; considering my leg and her deafness not a lot, but we were humbly grateful all the same. This wasn't easy to achieve in Boxgrove Avenue, Guildford in 1932, but many many years later Barbara committed suicide which may have been a kind of keeping of that long ago pact, a giving up on life as an offering.

One or two holidays I spent with my godfather, a schoolmaster who had once been in the army in Burma where he had met my mother. He was a devout Christian in the nicest possible way my Uncle Ernest, straight of back and ruddy of skin, who ran round the streets of Bromsgrove every morning and then jumped into a cold bath to keep in the "good fettle" of his army days. Twice he took me to Cornwall, and as we walked along the cliffs talked of "box wallahs" and "tamashas" and "badmarshes" beside the Irrawaddy. Nothing exciting had ever happened to him since then, but I couldn't give full attention to his stories because I was panting to keep up with him, who marched along as if in pursuit of bandits up a Burmese mountain.

Once or twice I went to Suffolk, to a farm run by friends of my brother. The days were long, the fields were flat, the farmer's placid wife left me to fill in the time as best I could. One holiday I remember well. I had progressed from surgical boots to special shoes, and because they were very expensive I only had one pair, for school and holidays, scuffed but serviceable. When we went out anywhere I was told to go and change my shoes. There was no way I could tell the truth, so sleepless nights were spent trying to plan how to make one pair of shoes look like two, or even three. I thought of dyes, and bows glued on. I invented lies about how I had lost my other pair, and pleaded stomach pains when it was time to change for church. The shame of being the possessor of only one pair of shoes was simply unbearable. I had given up asking for divine intervention by then.

When I asked my mother how she could have sent me to spend so many holidays with her sister Margery, she vowed there was no alternative. I was saved from going mad and being sent to Rampton by several interventions from my maternal grandmother. My grandmother's flat smelt of sandalwood and mothballs and a leathery, woody, dusty aroma arising from her bookcases, lacquer chests, brocade sofas and old albums. A dark corridor ran the length of the flat, only just passable because of the clutter of cabinets, ending in the sitting room and bedroom. It had a small kitchen, a tiny bathroom and another poky bedroom; cramped, five stories up, without a garden, absolutely wrong for a child, absolute heaven to me.

The day started with the arrival of the Daily Mrs Cooksley (except for the odd occasion when she had been beaten senseless by her drunken husband) and the carrying in of my grandmother's breakfast tray; a boiled egg under a knitted cosy, toast and tea. Afterwards Granny sawed her teeth with strong cotton and untied her hair so that if fell in orange corrugated waves on her shoulders. Then she brushed these a hundred times with her silver backed hairbrush, as ladies had to do, and I thought the golden shower very beautiful; until my mother complained one day of the common colour Granny dyed her hair, ridiculous at her age. My grandmother laboured with my rat brown tresses, wrapping them round a hot poker and then carefully slipping the poker out, leaving me with hot sausages resting on my shoulders.

Her ideal of feminine beauty being Queen Alexandra, she even tried a clothes peg on my drooping nostrils, but soon realised it was a waste of time. The long neck, the flaring nostrils, the heavily lidded deep set eyes would need a lot more than clothes pegs to achieve. Plain I was and plain I must stay, prominent teeth with iron bars across them not adding much to the picture of my ten year old self. She was vain of her own looks, and protected her skin with spotted veils and her hands with white shammy leather gloves. Hands were barometers of ladyhood and hers were daily oiled, the nails polished, the skin gently pushed back to reveal the moons. She had a manicure box with ivory tools which is still in my drawer, reminding me of a lost world.

You could always tell a lady by her hands was one of her frequent pronouncements, meaning that it was not at all respectable for them to look as if they had been used. Thick blue worms crawled all over the back of Mrs Cooksley's hands, and she hardly had any nails, let alone moons. This struck me as perfectly in order, though she was as old as my grandmother and might have been expected to be resting both hands and thick swollen legs, it was natural that instead she would use both in our service. When she wept over the sink, describing the previous night's beating, I played hopscotch on the lino tiles and thought nothing of it. The lower classes always had drunken husbands my grandmother said.

After breakfast and the teeth and hair rituals, my grandmother dressed, a long drawn out affair ending with the piling of her amber hair on top of her head, secured by copper coloured hairpins. While she dressed she talked of Burma, which came to smell to me of the creams and oils she rubbed into her precious skin, and the cologne she sprayed from the syringe shaped like a crinolined lady. Finally she drew on, finger by finger, her shiny gloves, easing them over her rings, perched on her gold head a hat with a spotted veil, and wound round her neck the fox with glass eyes permanently swallowing its own tail.

Before we set out we must remember to take with us the template of newspaper cut to fit a lavatory seat. It was very dangerous to use public toilets, and ladies were especially vulnerable to the diseases lurking there. Though we only went to the most respectable places; the Tate Gallery, the Natural History Museum, William Whiteleys, one could never be too careful. The nature of our danger was unmentionable, one of the many delicious mysteries surrounding women. Another was a hot water bottle with a long rubber tube attached to it that hung behind the bathroom door. It was part of that post-thirteen world when I would have several pairs of shoes, one of them pink satin; when my nostrils would flare, my eyes acquire lids, and a man with sweet smelling hands would promise me a future at his side on the mission field.

The days my grandmother and I spent carrying our newspaper templates around in our gloved hands were quite tiring for me, but she had the knack of turning every event into an adventure. When I dragged my leg back through the park, the Serpentine turned into the Irrawaddy, she being chased up it by the bandits which featured prominently in her stories. We always stopped at the same baker's shop and chose a cake each for tea, which we put on the plate Mrs Cooksley had left, with the orange and gold cups turned face down on their saucers. The fire was laid on a bed of paper rolls we had prepared the previous evening. These paper sausages didn't always catch, and then we had to take a sheet of the Morning Post and hold it in front of the smouldering grate and catch it back just before it caught fire and rose like an exploded airship up the chimney.

With the curtains drawn and the smell of burnt paper in our nostrils, we ate our cakes and then played patience or looked through albums at pictures of her sepia sisters, Minnie and Flo and Beautiful Beatrice of whom she talked, though now I have forgotten what she said. Morning and evening we prayed, kneeling in front of her brocade sofa, its scratchy surface smelling like everything in her flat of mothballs. On special occasions we opened the display cabinets and took out the Chinese boxes that fitted into each other, the ivory globe with endless other globes inside, the mother-of-pearl counters for eastern games. Before I went to bed Granny rubbed my leg with warm oil, and prayed for its cure. I added a silent postscript that He would stop the bedroom cupboard from creaking.

That cupboard was the only small cross I had to bear when I stayed with my grandmother Annie. The rest of the room was perfect; wallpaper with purple grapes hanging in bunches over trellises; an eiderdown covered with flowers and bright green leaves, an enchanted garden my fingers crossed each night, and on the wall a huge copy of Holman Hunt's "The Light of the World", the familiar Jesus of the scratched forehead and the white nightdress who had sat with me on the moors. But every night I was woken by the squeak of the cupboard door slowly opening, something unspeakably horrible poised to step out. During the day I confirmed that the cupboard held nothing but padded hangers with coats on them, and below a row of shoes held in shape by bits of wood and wire. And yet somewhere in the folds of the fur coats, something else lurked, a night creature who slowly pushed open the cupboard door however firmly I closed it, and who would lean over me and sink its yellow claws into my neck, Aunt Evelyn metamorphosed into a monster. Why didn't I tell Granny? The world of child and adult couldn't then, probably cannot now, be bridged.

My grandmother was a very literary lady, and members of Poetry Groups came to the flat for readings and tea. On these occasions we bought a Fuller's walnut cake and Mrs Cooksley donned a frilly apron to carry in the silver tray, tricked out with thin linen napkins and flashing with polished sugar tongs and slop basins. With her drooping eyes and neck I thought her starched cap made her look like one of the performing dogs at Bertram Mills Circus. I handed round the plates, my singed corkscrews tied back with a ribbon, feeling pretty and graceful in spite of my boots.

Some Sundays the Curate came and gave my grandmother communion, why I don't know since we walked miles round museums and art galleries every day, but perhaps there were times when she was "seedy" and couldn't get to church. Men of the cloth still mesmerised me, and this one was dark and handsome and took Father Orr's place in my daydreams. I awaited his arrival with beating heart and bobbing ringlets, and put him at the top of the list of men I would bewitch after I was thirteen. In preparation we covered the dining table with a white cloth, and placed on it candles and the family Bible; he brought the bread and wine. I wasn't allowed to witness the sacred rituals, not being confirmed, and sat in my bedroom staring at the "Light of the World" and expanding like a gas balloon. My grandmother often read me poetry and Walter de La Mare's traveller knocking on the old oak door became confused with Jesus, but in the nicest possible way. The door of my own heart was wide open to them all.

For two summer holidays my grandmother took my brother Richard and I to Seaford, where we spent our days with the Children's Special Service Mission. Each morning would find the three of us on the beach building a pebbly altar, round which we wrote "God is Love" in seaweed, and beside it a sandcastle onto which sprang young men and women in blazers to lead us in choruses and shout that we must open our hearts to the Lord Jesus, now, this very morning, this very moment. The wooden door of my heart, with the patient figure knocking on it while his horse was nearby on the forest's ferny floor, was rapturously ajar.

In the afternoons we went for treasure hunts, the clues of which were texts from the Bible, and in the evenings there were sausage suppers round a camp fire, when we sang mournful choruses; "Break Thou the Bread of Life" we intoned, quite different from "I'm H A P P Y cos I'm S A V E D" of the morning. Under the stars the balloon filled again, with love for Jesus and for one of the young men in blazers. My daydreams were of the pair of us going together to Burma as missionaries, he in his navy blazer, me with my flaring nostrils and deep set eyes, floating up the Irrawaddy to where my grandmother, ageless, would be waiting for us.

When my mother returned after three years, she came as a shock. Her absence had made me create a fantasy figure on the lines of Marmy in "Little Women". My friends had been regaled with stories of her gracious appearance and predictions of the gifts she would come bearing, so when a small stout woman in a brown overcoat turned up, with a paper bag of toffees, I was mortified. She couldn't have been very impressed with me either, my mouth full of metal, my body expanding sideways rather than upwards. She took me away from Furzedown and the heady delights of Petting and caterpillar scented lockers, and before she left for India again sent me to the school where I spent the happiest year of my childhood.

Wadhurst College was a beautiful house, set in rolling fields with woods which we could wander at will. It had as its headmistress Miss Mulliner, who had made her name at Cheltenham Ladies College and brought with her ideas about freedom, good food, warmth and fun, and the minimum of rules. She provided teachers as relaxed as herself. The Science mistress wore boucle two pieces threadbare under the arms from the constant clutching of her hands across her chest, when with cries of "Ladies, Ladies" she admonished us for turning the lab once more into smoky confusion. Matron was ancient and her bright brown wig was held down by a white cap. It was the aim of our lives to dislodge it, but this only happened once when her cap got screwed down into a bottle of Radio Malt. She shuffled very slowly round the dormitories on her vest-smelling routines, and was provided with an Under Matron to do the real work.

Miss Mulliner started our happy days by sweeping down a wide staircase to morning prayers, dressed in brightly coloured smocks over ankle length skirts, yards of amber beads and an enormous hat. On Speech Days she drifted round the grounds in this outfit looking for Rudyard Kipling who lived over the hill and was always invited as our special guest, but never turned up. At the performance we later gave in the school hall we dressed up as sailors, and peering over our hands demanded of our slightly bewildered audience where all the big steamers had gone to. Kipling might have been able to answer, but he was never there.

Like everything else in the school, religion was a relaxed affair, and the door of my heart became quite rusty on its hinges. On Sundays Miss Mulliner drove me to church in her Morris Minor because it was a long walk. Behind the wheel she became a different person, not the respected headmistress of two famous schools but the Fastest Woman on Wheels this Century. We shot round bends at an alarming angle, and arrived with a screech of brakes, just missing the Vicar. We always seemed to be late in spite of our rapid drive, and it was embarrassing having to follow Miss Mulliner up the aisle in front of the choir.

Everything about that year was charged with electric delight. I had friends, good food, warmth, laughter and teaching that stretched my mind. I had a close relationship with two trees outside my dormitory window, and a passionate involvement with the woods through which I was allowed to wander when the others went for walks. The One World Soul flowed through me every time I sat with my face pressed to the bark of a tree, taking the place of Jesus who had let me down once too often. When my mother came home and took me away from Wadhurst I accepted it like everything else incomprehensible but foredoomed in my life.

She sent me to my penultimate school near Guildford, which was as different from Wadhurst as it was possible to be, and its headmistress as unlike Miss Mulliner. Miss Symes was a tank-like figure with the profile of a Roman emperor on an old coin. Parents thought she had a "striking" face, but I longed for the sagging cheeks, the kindly mouth full of slippery teeth of Miss Mulliner. Her teeth occasionally fell out, but only into her amber beads. Miss Symes's armour plated body, tweedy and twin setted, moved down the dark corridors of St Catherine's with doomed precision. Meeting her suddenly round a corner was like finding a rocky mountain sprung up in your path.

She ran the school as if it was part of an Empire, with masses of rules to keep the plebs in their place and prefects like prison guards to Report on anyone who broke them. There were rules about sitting on radiators, running in passages, placing hands in pockets, talking in cubicles, holding hands. There were endless rules connected with the lavatories, which we called the Alps because they were even colder than the rest of the school. These were patrolled by Matron, a thin crackly woman with steely eyes who peered over the half doors to see What We were Up To. I think Lesbian goings-on were suspected, but none of us knew what the word meant and we simply used the Alps as a place to meet and talk when lessons got too tedious.

St Catherine's was a Church School and its austerities perhaps considered good for our souls. The dormitories were absolutely arctic with a wind from Siberia blowing the cubicle curtains about. My chilblained leg lay on the snow-cold sheets like a half cooked sausage, red and pulsating. It was of course forbidden to use a hot bottle or to climb into another's bed for warmth. Even to enter a friend's cubicle was wicked, and prefects were posted strategically down the long central aisle ready to Report on us for talking, especially After Lights Out, or creeping through a curtain to giggle with a friend.

If they saved on heating, they saved even more on food at this holy establishment. We had stringy stews, mostly watery gravy, and puddings the consistency of moist cement. The long tables at which we ate were numbered, and we had to pick little discs off a plate as we entered the dining room to show where we were to sit. C1 I dreaded since it landed me next to the Maths mistress with whom I had not one word to exchange, and we chewed our way through our pale brown stews in an embarrassed silence which seemed to go on for ever.

The whole structure of the school was based on the premise that unwatched we would be immoral at worst, at best comfortable and happy, not Christian conditions. Sundays were unspeakably dreary, thin fatty slabs of cold pork and beetroot for lunch, letter writing and mending in the evenings, and in between a long walk which I was excused. I sat alone in the Common Room, the grey light fading outside, my tongue exploring the roof of my mouth for fragments of pork fat. I tried to write a novel, but my hands were too cold, and it was risky because all writing including letters could be confiscated and read, and if found subversive could lead to expulsion. Being Expelled was a shame one would never live down. I remember us all standing in shocked silence while a girl was led down the front steps and into a waiting car and driven away as if to the guillotine. What crime she had committed to be thus expelled I can't remember, but it cast a gloom over us for days.

Yet as the years passed we grew rebellious my friends and I and refused to play lacrosse, or if we did dropped the ball on purpose so as to get Sent Off, and had permanent Periods to get off gym. My best friend and I planned to be famous authors and wrote endless plays modelled on Noel Coward which we hid under our gym tunics so that we crackled as we walked. Miss Symes hated me for my "critical attitude" though grudgingly told my mother I was the cleverest girl in the school, and vouchsafed me the scholarship I was never allowed to take. I have frequently relived the life I would have had if I had been allowed to go to Oxford instead of being taken out to India.

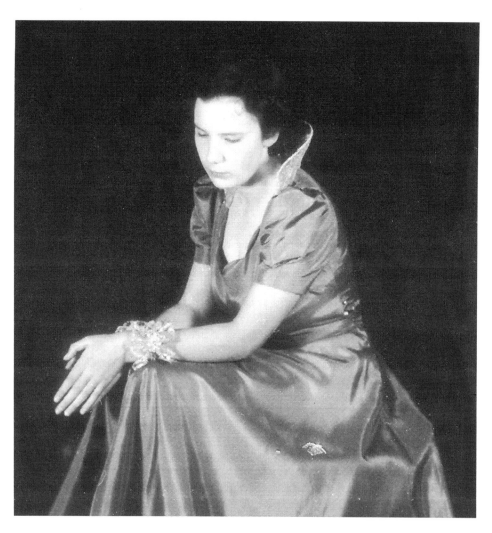

Iris in India before her marriage

My mother came home for the last time just after my sixteenth birthday, and sent me to my last school   She took a maisonette in Earls Court over a greengrocers shop, and I went daily by bus to an establishment in Queen's Gate dedicated to "finishing" girls and getting them ready to be presented at Court. We learnt interior decoration and flower arrangement, ladies coming from Fortnum and Mason and Constance Spry to demonstrate. We learnt how to write cheques and use make up. Most of all we learnt of our role in the world, to be submissive, elegant, feminine, a credit to our sex and attractive to the right kind of man. The other girls who were called Priscilla and Lavender and Charmian went along happily with this agenda. They talked a lot about Coming Out, and were swept away in chauffeur driven limousines. Sometimes they asked me back to tea in their gracious houses, and I dreaded one of them visiting me. Looking back dread was a word that cropped up a lot in my childhood.

118

Iris and Violet at Bareilly, 1939

I dreaded going to India, being lined up in front of men and for all the shortage of girls, being found too plain, too clever, too lame. But I submitted to spending the winter of 1938 being fitted by a dressmaker in Dorking with clothes to take for the boat and for all the parties and dances awaiting me Out There. Evening gowns were pinned round my lumpy figure; a chintz one like a chair cover; white net covered with green moons; black taffeta with a bolero to disguise my bust; white lace to wear at Government House. It would only be for a year of course. In fact it was for a lifetime.

IRIS: MARRIAGE

Mac in 1942

So on an April day in 1939 we walked up the gangway of the boat that was to Take Me Out, as my mother had been taken twenty three years before, as my own daughters would be taken twenty years ahead. All those headmistresses and aunts had led to this moment, as inevitable as it was frightening. For I remember being very frightened indeed at the prospect of having to play tennis and go to Tea Dances. I had got over some of the self-consciousness over my leg, but not all. I was sixteen and a half, and I thought it would be a long time, if ever, before an old, isolated I.C.S. man would have me.

We travelled Tourist Class which was odd, since my father was a Colonel by now and tourists were usually Tommies and Anglo Indians and very young Box Wallahs on their first tours. I hated the gangway from the First Class deck which brought down every evening a very pretty girl to dance with Roy, a medical student who made do with me till she arrived. Leaving them waltzing round the potted palms, I went out on deck and quoted Matthew Arnold: "Weary of myself and sick of asking, What I am and what I ought to be, At the vessels prow I stand which bears me Forward, forward over the restless sea." I wore a different dress nearly every night, but whether in chintz or green moons Roy dropped me like a hot coal as soon as Deirdre from First Class appeared.

Apart from Roy my only contact with a man was with a tea planter called Graham who showed me pictures of his estate, of monkeys and little bears, or so he told me because it was hard to tell from the underdeveloped prints. Little did I know that my life was to be spent in such a place, caring for similar creatures. My mother said Graham was dark and couldn't I find someone better to be friends with. She spent the voyage playing bridge, but sent me out every evening to dance and have fun. I didn't tell her that I spent most of the throbbing seductive hours with my chin on the ship's rail waiting for a non-appearing Roy.

Arriving in India then and always was dazzling and familiar. The smell of burnt gram and open drains, of sweat and spices, was carried in a warm breeze. The noise was deafening, the crowds jostled and shrieked, but in the days of Empire we white women had paths cleared for us and my mother's dalmatians. By that time she was a keen dog breeder and took out good specimens; hard for the dogs who slithered round the decks trying to find somewhere to relieve themselves; not particularly helpful in a country with millions of half-starved strays already.

We took a train up India for two days and nights. Of course we had a carriage to ourselves, and in the evenings unrolled our "bisters", canvas sausages that held our bedding, with pockets at each end for towels and a chamber pot. The dust rolled in clouds through the open windows and the studded leather seats grew slimy under our sweating thighs. At stations men handed in trays with teapots, and plates of bread covered with rancid butter, and little green bananas. Sunrises and sunsets were spectacular, and in my sticky corner I watched pass the country so long awaited, and wished never to arrive at the destination with dances and tennis courts.

The last stretch up into the Himalayas was in a taxi, round hairpin bends with dramatic dizzying drops, the air becoming cooler at each turn. My father met us in Naini Tal, at the hotel where we were to stay. My small brother, Robert, had been left in England at five years old; Billy was in the army and Richard heading for university. It was good to have a hot bath after the journey, in a tin tub filled from canisters carried by men on their shoulders. I soaked by lamplight, apprehension temporarily suspended in physical pleasure. Now I was to find out how my parents had been spending all those years while I was at my seven schools.

The first thing I discovered was that there was to be no settled home in India like the bungalow beside the Irrawaddy to which my mother had gone. The Raj were posted like mail-order parcels hither and thither from plains to hills, so that we never stayed anywhere longer than six months. During the two years before my marriage we lived in a hotel, two different bungalows and some rather superior tents. My mother was constantly packing, unfussed and in full song. "I dreamt I dwelt in mar-harble halls" echoed happily from the depths of tea chests as she stashed away the china and linen and the packets of letters from Harold and Arnold. Ant-like processions of coolies carried them up and down the hillsides on their backs, bent double, with straps round their sweating foreheads. When they stopped for a rest they laughed a lot and spat "pan" over the precipices. I later found out that they were sickly and short-lived.

Our departure from the maisonette in Earls Court had been hasty, almost furtive. It seemed we had been very short of the rent and had had to get away before an uncomfortable interview with the landlord. Now suddenly our fortunes were restored. We were staying in the best hotel in Naini Tal, the Royal, run by an elderly English couple and of course exclusively for Europeans. We had a chalet in the grounds with our own sitting room and went over to the hotel for meals, which were eaten to the accompaniment of a three piece band; two kinds of soup, fish, chicken, duck or pork with potatoes moulded into different shapes, soufflés, ice creams or gateaux, cheese and biscuits. A lot of the supplies must have been carried up by coolies who themselves lived on a handful of rice a day. Thoughts like that didn't occur to me until I had been in India for several years.

Naini Tal was very beautiful, its wooded hillsides rising steeply from a pear-shaped lake. For a few months I went to school, riding along the lakeside with the dalmatians streaming behind me. I still thought there was a chance that I would return home after a year, and maybe get to university. All Saints College had the necessary curriculum and was a friendly place. The other girls were either Indian or Anglo Indian, and my mother felt the same anxiety that Maria had felt as to whether I would pick up the accent, like some unpleasant disease. I wasn't allowed to join my schoolmates for curry lunches, but sat on the hillside eating hotel sandwiches. The idea of taking any of my friends to the hotel was unthinkable. I accepted this, like everything else, as a law of nature, fixed in the interests of us all.

There were twice weekly dances in the hotel, and I grew to dread Tuesdays and Thursdays because my mother couldn't bear to hear the band playing waltzes and fox-trots for other people to dance to, particularly for men who weren't dancing with me. Sometimes in desperation she would gather together the middle-aged grass widowers from surrounding tables, and get together a party for a dance. Nobody went without being in a party, and you had to stick with your own set for the evening. Both the Colonels and I found it hard work tramping round the wooden floor, from which the lounge carpets had been lifted for the evening. My silver slippers had high heels on which I could hardly balance, let alone dance.

The big social event was the Matelots Ball, run by the racing fraternity. My mother wangled a ticket for me, but when I arrived I found everyone else was in a party. My dance card dangled from my wrist embarrassingly bare. In the end one of the grass widowers took me over, and late on in the evening I got my first kiss in a cubicle under the boathouse. I was surprised but encouraged. He was only about forty and made me feel I could set my sights higher than district commissioners ready for retirement.

In September the war broke out, but this affected us very little. My small brother Robert was sent out, we all moved down to the plains, and in the Spring up to the hills again. The war brought a lot of young men in uniform on leave, and because I had thinned down a bit and girls were scarce, I started to have the good time that the East was famous for providing. My mother was pleased, but also jealous. There were barneys and long silent days. In the summer of the Battle of Britain I went to the YWCA to learn shorthand in the hopes of getting a job and leaving home.

But there was really nowhere to get away to, except into marriage, and at seventeen and a half I began seriously to size up my escorts. Four months after my eighteenth birthday I wore my black skirt and bolero to one more Boat Club dance and almost fell off my silver heels at the sight of a young man in our party, a brown-faced, golden-haired, blue-eyed Viking hero. I had fallen in love on an average once a month since arriving in India, but this time it was mutual. Unbelievably none of my drawbacks mattered: my leg, my non-flaring nostrils, my cleverness. My mother was equally astounded and lost no time in setting a date for the wedding.

But I had the same reservations and qualms as my mother had had. I wanted to marry; I hardly dared expect to be given another such chance; I was "in love" as who could help but be with such a man; I wanted very much to get away from home; but what about all the rest? What about university, and a career? Marriage would shut the door forever on all other relationships with men, so was this particular man going to satisfy me completely till the end of my days? Or me him come to that; I had learnt what adultery meant since my Furzedown days, but precious little else about sex or childbearing. After one of my hesitant days Mac sent me a letter like the one my father had sent my mother, with a kindly-phrased ultimatum: did I or did I not want to marry him, and if not would I please say so firmly and save both of us future trouble.

That clinched it, because I couldn't bear to see him walk away. My mother sent to convents in South India for beautifully embroidered underwear and the dhurzi sat on the verandah from dawn till dusk running up my trousseau, including my wedding dress, a foaming net and organdy affair which cost twenty rupees. My wedding in March was exactly like my mother's, an archway of crossed swords outside the church, rose petals thrown by little girls in satin dresses. Bareilly had an English church and an Archdeacon to marry us, though he wouldn't have been my first choice. He was lean and mean and worldly; you could set your watch by his afternoon walk to the cinema. He married us in his socks as he had an ingrowing toenail, and asked for his fee while we were signing the register.

Our honeymoon in Jaipur was like my mother's too: very hot and five days into it I got my period and that was the last one until my son was born. Jaipur was beautiful, its wide streets tramped down by camels, with peacocks as common as sparrows, and its people tall and graceful in brilliant floating garments. Its buildings of red sandstone were full of history, but neither of us knew any Indian history so we couldn't appreciate them. We were as happy as two people could be who had lived rootless lives. Mac's parents had left him at school in Scotland at the age of twelve and returned to Mexico to work, and he had been sent out to plant tea at nineteen. Now he was twenty-three, I was eighteen and we both felt needed, loved, settled. It was like opening the door of my grandmother's flat and smelling the comfortable, safe smell of sandalwood and mothballs.

Wedding in Bareilly 1941

124

*

Nothing in fact could have been less settled than the future, and I shudder at our effrontery at facing it so confidently; the thought of Mac being almost immediately killed had never entered into my calculations as to whether I would marry him. He had joined up as soon as he could and was with a brigade getting ready to go to Singapore to fight the Japanese. Then he heard a regiment was to be raised in Assam, where he planted tea, and applied to join it. The hill peoples who would form the regiment were the Mongolian tribes of the wooded mountains circling the Brahmaputra Valley, and renowned for their skill in jungle warfare, and for their intelligent and cheerful natures. They would make wonderful soldiers and had the advantage of looking quite like the Japanese in dark jungle.

Everyone said how lucky I was to be going to Shillong in northeast India which was just like Scotland, they said, pine forests and heather and sparkling brooks. The journey to reach it was five days long, and I did it alone with a Siamese kitten as Mac had gone ahead to make arrangements for our accommodation. As I sat in the train feeling sick in my early stages of pregnancy, I was delighted with the country that rolled past the windows, but after two years I was still a tourist. I knew nothing, absolutely nothing about either its past or present. I had seen the Taj Mahal, and the Himalayan snows under sunset and moonlight. I had ridden in the early morning through villages round Bareilly and watched women slapping chapattis on stones, or bending, graceful as birds, to fill their water pots. Now from the train I watched men plodding over enormous landscapes behind bullocks, and at stations sighed over the huddled homeless, the pinched children and mangy dogs. Poor creatures, so dreadfully poor, but better off in some unexplained way for having us the British there.

India was for me, as it had been for my mother and for my great grandmother Maria, a backdrop to the life of the cantonment, which was games, dances, dinner parties, tame ponies on which to amble down sandy paths of a morning for a picturesque glimpse at how "they" lived. Now India was at war, on our side naturally, in spite of Gandhi and Nehru trying to cause trouble. It seemed perfectly proper to persuade tribal peoples down from their hills, to train them to fight for us and in many cases die in our cause. They were not being forced after all, only being offered more money than they had ever seen to do what came naturally to them.

The Indian army had employed my family for several generations; now I was temporarily an army wife. I had no thoughts about the war that was being waged except that it was inevitable and righteous and that we would win it, we always did. Mac looked very handsome in uniform and was very happy too with his new recruits, jolly little men who did tribal dances on mess nights, jumping about with their spears, with hornbill feathers in their hair. Shillong was indeed beautiful, and its indigenous people, the Khasis, delightful. The women wore hoods of handwoven wool, and sat by the roadsides roasting corn in iron pans and laughing a lot through betel-stained lips. The climate was perfect, the flowers in the cottage

125

gardens enormous, and in the centre of the town there was a lake round which grew beds of brilliant cannas. It was hard to remember what we were there for, war seemed remote, we were safe and happy.

We would be happier still once our new home was built on the outskirts of the town. Meanwhile we shared a bungalow with another young couple called Les and Joan. It had open drains running past the door and a kitchen black with flies, but we could bear it for a few months, until our wooden chalet was ready for us in the pine woods of Happy Valley. A lot of our wedding presents had been broken in the journey over, and we only had a couple of armchairs and a frayed carpet in the sitting room, but as my sickness left me, and my baby stirred, I felt placid and fulfilled. I knitted and planned and walked through the laughing rows of Khasi women between the heavy monsoon showers. No barneys, no disappointing my mother. Mac assured me he loved me more each passing day that I swelled beneath my floral smocks. We had very little money but were cocooned by love and relief that the other was there.

There were only two other regimental wives, Joan and the colonel's wife. The officers were tea planters like Mac, chosen because they had lived in Assam and been members of the Assam Valley Light Horse, a sort of police force run by the tea firms, presumably originating from the wild and unsettled state of the early planting days. It was a remarkable regiment; remarkable in the composition of its men from high mountains who spoke no English and often no Assamese or Urdu and who had no quarrel with the Japanese; remarkable in the intended speed with which it was going to turn such men into soldiers, dress in khaki those who had only worn beads and penis pouches, teach them to handle guns and send them into action against a sophisticated enemy. Tea planters were not perhaps the best people for the job, and the colonels chosen to co-ordinate the whole operation a very curious collection.

The first colonel was a flamboyant career soldier, who thought of the job as a necessary if boring step along the road to G.H.Q; the second a weak and ineffectual misfit; the third a sour and bitter Gurkha passed over by his own regiment; and the fourth a religious maniac and misogynist who left the army to become ordained. How this motley crew came to be selected I can't imagine. It says a lot for the character and intelligence of the hillmen that they turned rapidly into soldiers second to none. On their prowess and courage largely depended the resistance that turned back the Japanese at Kohima.

In that first year as an army wife I was still conditioned to think that I was in a splendid institution whose rules, though a bit like those of Miss Symes, yet reflected the necessities of a long, golden tradition. When the colonel ordered us to turn up every Saturday night at the mess, I dutifully did so in my chiffon maternity dress and sat on a hard chair listening to his stories of communications from his great friends in Delhi, who apparently tapped eternally on morse sets to tell him how wonderful he was. A lot of his time in Shillong was spent making more friends: with the Governor and his Lady, the Chief Commissioner and the Inspector General of

126

Police. What they had all said to each other during the previous week was our Saturday night's entertainment.

The mess was a wooden hut decorated with painted wooden rhinos, which were the regimental crest, and occasionally some of the colonel's luminous chums were persuaded to join us there. Then the tribal men were called in to dance for them. This was interesting, but made me feel vaguely uncomfortable. The real purpose of the dances, warlike or religious, had gone. For these young soldiers it was probably the first time they had been presented with the fact that their private rituals were a source of amusement to white men.

Naga war dances started quite quietly, but gradually worked up to a pitch of excited stamping and whooping that got them ready to go off and collect heads. The colonel didn't consider it seemly to allow the dancers at the mess to reach such a state; perhaps all those smiling white faces might be a temptation. At a certain point he waved a lordly hand to bring the dance to a halt, and the long line of bronzed men stopped leaping and shouting and waving their axes, and shuffled off.

In the Autumn, the big festival of Dasseera was an occasion for invited guests at an outside entertainment, seated on a row of chairs behind a trestle table on the sports ground. Mac was away on a course when the invitation arrived - it was more a command - to attend the Dasseera celebrations. I think he would have forbidden me to go and told the colonel of the likelihood that I would go into premature labour at what I would have to witness. As it was, ignorant and still conditioned to do what a good army wife should, I sat all afternoon watching goats and bullocks being dragged into an arena to have their heads cut off, and their bleeding corpses lugged round to loud cheers. I became violently agitated and wanted to leave, but the colonel in the front row, flanked by his important friends, shook his head and flapped his hand, ordering me back to my seat. I put my head in my hands and wondered for the first time if the army was really right about everything.

At the next mess night I was taken aside and reprimanded for my behaviour, which might have caused offence, the colonel said, to the wielders of the bloody axes. Cementing the Regimental Spirit was an important part of his task, and this meant respecting the troops and their customs. I didn't say that as far as I was concerned they were entitled to their customs, but I saw no reason why I should have to take part in them. I hung my head dutifully and blamed my condition for my nauseated reaction. He was patronisingly kind, and handed me over to his wife, a gentle and subservient woman who had sat through years of bloody rituals on his behalf, and she told me I would get used to such things, which were part of army life.

It was at that point that the army, the provider of splendid careers for my family, began to be revealed to me as a lot of stupid rather vain men, working a system based on sycophancy, snobbery, ambition and bullying. I was making the same discoveries as Harold had done in his hut in Folkestone; and I made them bit by bit but with ever increasing assurance. I could afford to take the long view, since I was married to a temporary acting soldier. Luckily, I didn't know that tea plantations were run on the same lines: the using of a presumed inferior, poorly paid and under-rated set of people for ends that would greatly enrich their employers. The skills expected of leaf-pluckers were less than those of army recruits so they were treated much worse, but at least didn't have to go off and die for obscure reasons.

Soon after Dasseera we moved into the wooden house built a few miles outside Shillong in a beautiful, unspoilt situation aptly named Happy Valley. The houses were scattered amongst pine trees and smelt of newly split wood, a great improvement on the open drains. The soil around them was bright red, and they backed onto moors covered in lentana bushes which in Autumn were laden with red and gold berries. I didn't tell Mac about my doubts about the army, which he never shared, and for the moment was indeed delighted with what it was offering me. I wheeled my second-hand pram up and down the wooden verandah, hardly noticing the bombing of Pearl Harbour.

On a night of thick mist five days before Christmas I started my pains, and Mac tried without success to start the hired car that was to take me the seven miles into hospital. Eventually he roused some of his men to push, and while they laughed and heaved I sat in a ditch groaning. I had no idea what to expect, having attended no ante-natal clinics; the spacing of pains meant nothing and when we finally reached hospital I was put into a room alone with the cheerful information that it was going to get a lot worse before it got better.

An hour later when someone popped in to see me there was panic, a lot of noise, shouts to go and get the doctor, banging of enamel bowls, creaking of trolleys as I was wheeled helter-skelter to the operating theatre. The lady doctor, a European in this largely Indian-women-only hospital, rushed in rather tousled and put a pad of chloroform over my face. My son, Alan, was born rather blue with forceps marks on his forehead and because I was unconscious I still didn't know exactly what had happened.

Compared to my mother's stories, my own about this first delivery was quite tame. I had a room to myself, specially reserved for paying white patients, the hospital was clean, the Khasi nurses gentle and cheerful. And yet I was left alone for an agonising and frightening hour during my first confinement. Nobody gave me advice or encouragement, and afterwards the baby was dumped with me to feed and removed again to a strictly timed routine. I had stitches and breast abscesses and didn't put a foot to the ground for ten days. It was not at all what I expected; it was a messy, uncomfortable experience, vaguely degrading. I worried about my little bluish baby who wouldn't take the vast amount of milk I had to offer. Looking back, I feel I was lucky not to end up like Poor Aileen.

However, I didn't get post puerperal depression, nor was I more than passingly depressed by the news. I only vaguely responded to the disastrous events further east: the fall of Singapore, the sinking of the Prince of Wales and the Reliant. For me, it was mustard coloured stools that mattered, and whether Alan had put on the required four to six ounces a week. I had a book called "Modern Methods of

Feeding in Infancy and Early Childhood" which I treated like Holy Writ, and lay awake listening to my starving baby's screams at night because of the page where it said, underlined in black, "on no account give night feeds".

I think of those four months in Happy Valley as an oasis in the long, arid stretch of war that was the first four years of my marriage. Our wooden floors were uncarpeted, and the little furniture we could afford we rented from a Chinaman. The month Alan was born our entire pay packet went on hospital fees, and no month was easy. Yet to run our four-roomed house we had a cook, bearer, sweeper, water carrier, ayah and gardener, the absolute minimum of servants on which one was expected to manage. My part in the running of the house was to sit in front of my desk in the morning, writing in my Memsahib's Account Book. Here in the appropriate columns went the daily cost of sugar, flour, chickens and Vim powder; the latter must have been used for some esoteric rites because we got through several tins a week.

My Ayah was one of the hooded Khasi women; she pattered about on bare brown feet, gentle and spotless, and hung nappies up between the pine tree branches. My book had said that I must get a screen and a table for the bath so a Chinaman made these for me, and I sat and fed Alan for long hours behind the screen, inexpertly so that he had too much or too little and was restless. He grew a little, but not as fast as the book said he should, and my heart sank at every weighing. The advance of the Japanese armies towards our borders worried me less than what the scales would reveal.

And then quite suddenly our pine clad paradise looked like becoming a trap. If the Japanese crossed into India, they would be able to cut us off. For a few weeks we wavered, and then Mac decided to send us away. Perhaps he had some information he couldn't reveal. We told one another that it was just for a while, just until things calmed down. In fact it was four years before we were back, four long, rootless years of trailing about India, waiting for leaves, waiting till the war ended. The sense of suspension, of stagnation, experienced in wartime is impossible to describe. Every sentence began and ended "when it's over" the bit in between aimless and constricted, like being on remand.

The April day we chose to leave Assam was the same one decided on by about a third of its population. I was travelling with Alan in one basket, and a Siamese cat with four kittens in another, clothes, tins of Ostermilk, and nobody to help me. This seems extraordinary when I think of it now. I was nineteen years old and had a five day journey ahead of me and yet no servant or orderly could be spared to come with me even as far as Calcutta. I suppose we relied on the usual obsequious station master to clear the way for me, lead me to a first class carriage, dust down the seats and lock the door against intruders. That was the usual procedure, but these were unusual events and normality was abandoned. I was just one of thousands fighting my way out of a beleaguered position.

Mac didn't even come with me to the boat, where I crossed the Brahmaputra to reach the railhead. I had to fight my way up the gangway, and then stand jammed to the rails, unable to move for the crowds. A servant passed carrying a tray above his head, and as he fought his way through the press of people I was able to remove the fish from the plate and drop it into the cat's basket. There was no question of feeding Alan, it was all I could do to stop him being trampled underfoot. Off the boat, we were ten deep on the platform waiting for the train. When it pulled in, its doors remained firmly shut. It was already crowded and was obviously going to pull out again quite quickly without taking on any more passengers.

And then a miracle occurred. A white arm, a hand with scarlet glistening nails attached to it, beckoned me from a crack in a window. Somehow I got myself over to the door, and it opened, and I was back in the world I knew: a first class compartment with only one other passenger, a Memsahib with her bister and her case of soda water bottles and her bearer crouching in the lavatory door. I gave no thought to the crowds abandoned on the platform as we slid out. They were used to being treated like this. Like the working classes of my grandmother's time, they would feel perfectly at home on station platforms, refused entry to the last train out.

I was speechless with gratitude to the lady who had let us in, and the cat and I both settled down to feed our offspring. She carrying hers between her teeth under the seat and managing better than I did. In all the heat and stress I had little milk, but this wouldn't be a serious problem as I could get boiling water from the engine to make up a bottle. For the moment Alan was pacified and we sat in a clammy, contented heap in the corner of the carriage and listened while our companion declared what an impossible place India was, and now it talked of Independence, as if it could run itself when it couldn't even run its trains in a civilised manner.

She took a spray from her pigskin vanity case and freshened her face with Eau de Cologne, and then while she ate peaches, peeling them with a silver-handled knife, told me that her husband was a prominent member of Calcutta's business community and would see to it that someone would be hauled over the coals for this disgraceful shambles. When the train pulled in at stations, she pulled down the blinds and closed her eyes wearily at the noise of hammering fists and cries of supplication.

I lifted a corner of the blind at the third station, and then went to let in an English family while she was sighing behind her lowered lids. She was so angry at the presence of two more adults and a child that she withdrew into her corner with her soda water, and refused to share a drop of it with any of us, though she gave a bottle to her bearer. We had to step over him to use the lavatory, which we did as little as possible as it was filthy and waterless.

The couple I had let in allowed me to share their provisions since I had relied on the trays coming through the window. These never appeared, nor was there anyone to go up and get boiling water for bottles and my milk became a tiny trickle. Alan moaned and sweated, but when we reached Calcutta the following evening it was I who was in a state of heat exhaustion, staggering and retching. My companions said I was in no state to travel on as I had intended, and led me and my baskets to a car and drove us all to their flat. Our haughty fellow traveller was met by a liveried chauffeur and stepped into an enormous limousine, leaving her bearer to find his own way with the crate of soda water.

Alan was given a bottle of milk, I was given iced lime juice and the cat a plate of fish. Then I was laid to rest in an air-conditioned room, and when I woke, I showered and ate steamed chicken and slept again. I can still remember the exquisite sense of relief, physical and mental, and by the morning my milk was back and I was ready to continue my journey. For the next day and night I was provided with a paraffin stove to boil water, which I could do alone in my first class carriage since all the other evacuees had ended their journeys at Calcutta. I never saw the family again but their care of me might well have saved my life.

I thought of that first half of my trip as something exceptional, fearful and unrepeatable. It didn't occur to me that Indians always travelled like that, except that they would be packed solid in their carriages, seven a side on slatted benches. So very long it took me to shake off my Jones assumptions, that the lower classes and the coloured races didn't "feel" things the same way, having simple nervous systems like lobsters.

I went back to my mother in Naini Tal, thinking it would be a short stay, but after I left, Shillong became a closed area to all but military personnel. However, when Mac became dangerously ill after two operations - we had both got appendicitis on the same day at opposite ends of India but I recovered more quickly - I made the journey back to see him without being challenged. This time I left Alan and the cat behind, and though only recently out of hospital, there were no crowds and there were men with trays and I was comfortable and segregated in the way I expected. I was worried sick though, as during those four days I had no idea what was happening to Mac. The telegram that had reached me simply said that he had been put on the danger list after his operation.

He was alive when I reached the Mission Hospital, but unrecognisable, gaunt like an old man. In the relief at seeing me, the abscess that was still keeping him feverish burst, and he started to heal. All round him, wall to wall in the rooms and all down the corridors, were sick and wounded from the Burma campaign. His appendix couldn't have chosen a worse moment to erupt, to turn septic, and then lead to jaundice. The two mission doctors were working round the clock; one of them had himself recently walked out of Burma, but they were always calm and cheerful. Later, one of them was to deliver my second daughter.

I had to find somewhere to live near the hospital, and was told of an American lady, who let rooms. When I went to see her I discovered that her husband was a Khasi, and called himself Reverend, since they had founded between them a fundamental type church: The One True Only Church of God. As far as I could judge they were the Two True Only Members, along with their hump-backed servant girl and their three sons. The Reverend and his sons ran a soft drinks business, but its profits, if any, didn't come into the house. She and I lived on pigeons' legs perched on a few grains of rice, which I supplemented with corn cobs bought off the Khasi stalls.

She lived in a fantasy world, driven there, I suspected, by her husband's neglect. He only made rare visits to the house, so was replaced in her affection and thoughts by her Daddy-God. In the evening she took off her red wig and let down her thin, greying hair and sang me the hymns that Daddy had dictated to her during the day. "Beautiful, beautiful are the children of the true church, beautiful beautiful are their lips, their hands, their eyes, their feet," she wailed softly in the light of the flickering paraffin lamp. I listened drowsily and explored my teeth for fragments of pigeon. Meals were not only scant, but often interrupted by sudden messages from on high, which would make her leap to her feet and speak in tongues. These coded dialogues with God surprised me at first, but soon became part of high tea.

When the Reverend did appear, we were both silent in his presence, she because she was frightened of him, I because I didn't know how to deal with his soft, insulting banter. "Such an honour," he would drawl, "to have an English lady at our table. You English are fighters for our freedom isn't it?" How lucky Indians were, he mused, to be fighting their masters wars, driving their railway trains, running their sewage farms. He himself had an uncle who had been sent home to England and shown forty seven sewage farms, fortunate man.

Now I can sympathise with his feelings, and the probable insults his half-caste sons had had to endure, but at the time I found him unpleasant, and harboured suspicions that he might be a spy. During our lamplit gossips his wife often warned me about the lusts of married men, and how wives should always keep the key of the bedroom strapped to their bodies. The Reverend never shot a remotely lustful look in either of our directions.

My days were peacefully routine: a morning walk across a meadow to the hospital; an afternoon sleep to the thud of rain on the tin roof; another evening saunter to see Mac, the moistened air filled with the smell of burnt corn. Mac improved rapidly; and I didn't mention a slight problem of my own, the fact that my wound had opened and was oozing pus. I covered it with cotton wool, and only occasionally felt real discomfort. One afternoon I woke from my sleep to a great sense of peace all over, no itching or aching from my side. I looked down to see an inch of pink rubber tube protruding from my scar, part of the tube that had drained me and had been overlooked. After its removal I had no more trouble. I don't suppose it was the first piece of software to go missing in a British Military Hospital.

A few days before we left, Mac was able to walk very slowly across the field to the house and visit my room. We lay together on the bed, too weak too make love, but close in a way that had to last a long time. The war was out there, but here on a lumpy mattress we hoped so terribly for the best. We had no money, no home, an uncertain future, a very short shared past; but happiness was the circle of arms and the rain on the roof; if Alan had been with us, we would have hoped to stay like that forever.

In fact I only saw Mac once a year for the rest of the war; a couple of sweet, unreal weeks when we talked of "after the war" as of an almost impossible dream. We would go home and live in the country on some unspecified income. Mac had an uncle whose death he thought was going to release large sums of money, so "when Uncle Robert dies" became the first verse of our own, new ballad. We knew we would never subject our children to the separations we had suffered. Mac had spent his holidays as a boy with relations in Edinburgh in whose icy house Everyone quarrelled and lectured and saved string.

I travelled to Quetta to have my daughter, Fiona, repeating my mother's journey across the Sind desert in the fifth month of pregnancy. My father was stationed there and there was a chance that Mac would get on a Staff College course, so I set off on another of the three day train journeys that were an everyday part of life in India. This time, being pregnant, I hired a servant to help me, a man of whom I knew nothing except what his references told me, but we all knew that references were written by professionals according to standard rules and not to be relied.

Indian trains had no corridors, and yet I was perfectly happy to share a carriage for hours on end with an unknown Indian who could slit my throat, steal my money and disappear without the slightest chance of being caught. I could, and did, allow this stranger to take Alan for walks along the platforms absolutely trusting him not to let stray dogs or beggars touch his charge, without even a passing thought that he would kidnap him. At the end of the journey I paid him his wages and sent him back without a word of thanks, like a drover's dog.

I treated all servants like that. The Gurkha ayah who took Alan for walks on her back, washed his clothes, played with him patiently and inventively for hours on end, I sacked straight away when she asked for a rise in her tiny salary. In Shillong, I let the police remove the bearer and beat him half to death because I thought he had stolen a few rupees from my purse. He crept back, bruised and shaking, and picked up his belongings wrapped in a cloth and walked away without a word of reproach, innocent but cowed. Goodness, if he had complained I would have reported him to the police again.

We all thought we were good to our servants; servants loved their Sahibs we claimed, as we measured out the spoonfuls of rice and arrived home at three in the morning expecting to find the entire staff there to give us a meal. In fact, we treated them as a sub-species, barely human, certainly without feelings. Young English women screamed at men old enough to be their fathers, who could never answer back. Drunk young men at the bar shouted and cursed staff old enough to be their grandfathers. Nobody that I can remember ever said thank you. I mourn for all those mannerless years and find little excuse for myself.

Quetta is in Baluchistan, then on the edge of India, high and cold and bare except that when watered and warmed by the spring and autumn sun it burst into amazing flower and fruit; apricots and grapes, dahlias and daffodils, walnuts and wallflowers, everything grew in Quetta between being frozen by the kojak winds of winter and being boiled by the summer sun. Its people were tall and hawk-like, men and women of the high passes, as different as they could be from the golden-skinned, slant-eyed Khasis. I don't know why it had been chosen by the British for their staff college, being remote at the end of a long, desert train journey;

perhaps its emptiness made it right for route marches and firing off guns. In the war when I was there, it was a fairground. Every night was party night; non-stop we danced and drank and celebrated, though with small reason. Famine in Bengal could be brushed aside, but the war not.

Many couples met for this one year together and were jubilantly happy and in love. I was invited to take part in the fun and frolics. I was twenty two and as pretty as I was ever going to be. The dry air seemed to act as an aphrodisiac, and there was the usual ratio of fifty men to one woman so it was like one long Paul Jones, with a rush of men to capture the spare women when the music stopped. Perhaps if there had been contraceptive pills available I would have lost my head and had an affair, but I was too petrified of becoming pregnant even to contemplate it; within marriage it was a nagging worry, outside it - a nightmare.

Quetta was totally army, everyone was in uniform, even a lot of the women. After a few months I got a letter from one of the top brass saying I wasn't pulling my weight in the war effort, that I should leave my children with the ayah as did other wives, and work in the Bomber Shop. This was a craft shop whose proceeds went towards winning the war, and was always over-staffed. I wrote back and said my children were more important than the war, and that I considered it sufficient that my husband was likely to lose his life in the Cause. Perhaps this cheeky missive stopped Mac getting posted to Quetta, because that was the way the army worked. A friend who was beautiful and sophisticated and spent a busy year entertaining the right people was rewarded by having her husband posted to Brigade Major, Quetta.

When we weren't whooping it up at the club or mess, we went out into the country on extravagant shooting parties, with crates of whisky and hampers of food and a regiment of servants and beaters. I don't know who paid for all this, perhaps the proceeds of the Bomber Shop. We lit crackling fires and sang under the stars as in the Seaford days. Quetta was bitterly cold in the winter, and the poor got frostbite because of lack of fuel, but we always had plenty. The sweeper came round the house in the morning lighting fires in every room. I remember him squatting in his cotton rags in front of the newly lit logs, and holding up his thin hands for a moment or two before moving on. Strange how that image has stayed with me so clearly, and yet at the time it was nothing special, sweepers always wore rags poor creatures.

There was always something to celebrate in Quetta, you would have thought we were in the middle of a peace time boom instead of half way through a tricky war. We climbed into fancy dress for any reason at all: a birthday, the bombing of Dresden, a second front opened, and at last, two years after I had fled Shillong, the defeat of the Japanese at Kohima. There was an all night binge when these fantastic new bombs were dropped on Hiroshima, and the peace that followed called for streamers all over the club for a week under which parties continued without a pause.

So at last it was over, and I was in another train going back to Shillong, across the Sind desert, a stop in Calcutta, and then up through Bengal and over the

Brahmaputra along with two children and a labrador puppy my mother had given me as a parting present. She had gone home, and my father was to follow a year later, their long commitment to India over. After my marriage my relationship with my mother was easier, I could busy myself with the children during the day and go partying at night without in any way disturbing her life; in fact, for the first time I was measuring up to the standards expected of me. She provided me with a home and solid support when I was ill; I nearly died of jaundice in Quetta and during that time she was a rock of comfort and practical help; she was always at her best when things became difficult.

Unexpectedly, I found myself an obsessive mother, and every waking moment of my children's day was spent amusing them. Alan had developed what was then known as acidosis and was frequently sick, and had two bouts of dysentery, so was a constant worry. Without my mother's help I don't know how I would have coped. I think I took all this for granted, saying thank you seems to have come hard for me all my life.

Back in a wooden hut in Happy Valley, I was soon pregnant again but no matter, the war was over, the dream had unbelievably come true. Mac was stationed in the plains but managed to get up for odd weekends. He had had a frustrating war from his point of view: the first battalion he raised went off to distinguish themselves at Kohima and he was left behind to raise another, but by that time the Japanese were in retreat and he only lingered on the fringes of action. He never spoke of the war afterwards, I think he felt faintly ashamed of his lack of having anything exciting to say.

Mac brought up a little pony for the children, and we sauntered across the parade ground in long domestic trails; children, horse, dog, ayah and my swelling self, choosing if possible a time when the colonel would be inspecting his men. Once we managed to do it when General Auchinleck was up on a visit, a masterpiece of timing. This effort at embarrassing the colonel was to repay him for putting my bungalow out of bounds to his officers, this being the holy misogynist who apparently saw me, bulbous as I was, as a biblical harlot. Fortunately, one of them ignored his orders and helped me get coal and gave me lifts into the shops in one of the fleet of army jeeps. Happy Valley was miles from anywhere and there were no buses.

My second daughter, Anne, was born in the hospital to which I had walked every afternoon across the field full of the smell of burnt corn; I never went back to visit my old landlady for reasons I now forget. Uncle Robert was still alive, so there was nothing to do but to go back to planting tea. We still talked about chucking it all in and getting that rose-covered cottage, but it was a bit like getting to be thirteen and finding my leg cured. Gradually, imperceptibly the dream thinned, faded and was gone. Instead there were to be twenty years of tea planting, and a repetition of all the long separations of our childhoods.

Luckily, life presents itself in pieces; the whole panorama doesn't spread itself in front of you like one of Mac's army maps: the hidden pitfalls, the long featureless plains, the sharp rocks, the deep jungles, the hills almost too high to surmount, none of these is apparent beforehand, only after when there is nothing more to be done. As I set off on yet another train journey, only a day this time, up the Brahmaputra valley newly planted with rice and steaming between monsoon showers, I felt nothing but relief at the thought of having a permanent home at last.

IRIS: TWENTY YEARS IN TEA

When I rounded the corner and saw the big, rambling bungalow perched on stilts, climbed over by flaming shrubs, many-doored, dark-roomed, huge, it was a relief. For me, though, there was less of disappointment and more of relief. I had a husband I loved and three children to occupy me so the isolation of the tea garden was not a great problem. I weighed six stone after my years in India and my many minor illnesses and one major one, and three births, and a lot of stressful wandering of the continent. Each hot day entirely engrossed me, and I only collapsed occasionally into a wicker chair on the verandah to watch the huge black hornets nesting in the greenery above. One sting would probably have killed a child, but it never occurred to us to disturb them, nor they us.

Looking back at the self that I then was, twenty four years old with seven years of India behind me and a great deal more in front, I find it hard to approve. I still knew nothing of the country outside the bungalow and club; had the barest command of its language; had shifted imperceptibly from my rigid white woman's stance in that I was beginning to feel a need to explore, but only on my own terms; had been original only in my rejection of the values of the army but even then with a response that was personal and trivial. I was still a Jones to my bigoted bones. Yet somewhere there must have been seeds of discontent lying, ready to sprout when the right rain fell on them. Now, from old age, I sometimes wonder if they would have been better left dry. Their stunted half-growth was failure and disappointment.

Wetness was the thing I remember about my first experience of Assam; the whole country was awash, and half the population seemed to be sitting on their roofs waiting for the floods to subside. Every year the monsoon rains washed away the bamboo bridge across the river that connected us with the club, sometimes carrying away the odd car or cow since there was no knowing the precise moment it would collapse. Then you had to cross in a dug out canoe, skillfully maneuvered over the foaming water by a very old man with a pole. Mac did this every week to play polo, but I was nervous, with a pair of toddlers and a suckling infant, and waited for the building of the new bridge which would signal the start of the social season.

While I waited I learnt things about tea planters that surprised and shocked me. We were "acting" as manager for a couple who had spent the war more or less unsupervised, and every empty space around the bungalow and below it in cavernous go-downs, was stashed with booty collected from the U.S. army; jeeps, fridges, tinned food, crates of whisky, you name it and they were ready to sell it to you for ten times its value. Their herd of cows was fed free, the milk from them skimmed and then sold back to the hospital. Manure was brought up in lorry loads to the vegetable garden, and the mountains of cabbages and tomatoes that resulted (tended by free labour) were also sold. Nothing in fact was paid for; servants, stores, kerosene, coal, they were all "written off" in ways that we had to follow while we were there. It was so easy to cheat on a tea garden that the word lost its meaning and it was considered quaint to use it. Yet we continued to watch our servants like hawks and count the cigarettes in their silver boxes before we went to bed.

Christmas was a bonanza, every handshake concealed a gold coin and we sat in the club comparing our presents: the silks and jewels, the farmyards of geese and ducks and goats given us by contractors who hoped to get our custom. It wasn't bribery I was told, it was "dastur", habit, custom, the whole of India was run on it and it was not for us to interfere. So I stifled my conscience, and when we went on leave I took the gold coins to money changers in Calcutta who sat behind bars in the bazaar and tested them between their teeth before handing me a wad of notes. Some people melted the gold and made it into jewellery instead.

The club, when I could get to it, was a small wooden building with a pale green field in front - the polo Ground - and three tennis courts at one side. It was provided inside with scratched bamboo chairs along the walls, and two bars, one for men only. There was nothing for the children to do, no swings or sandpits, not even a tree to climb. After the games were played by the adults, the men retired to the billiard room and their private bar, and the women sat in a circle and talked about their servants. The children sagged on my lap, pale and hungry, and we were all of us too tired to be nervous of Mac's erratic driving over the creaking bamboo bridge on the way home. But I still lived in the present. I don't remember thinking, "This is how I shall be spending my leisure hours for the next twenty years".

Alan, Iris, Anne and Fiona at Cherideo Tea Estate, Assam, 1958

138

Meanwhile Uncle Robert died, but there was no money after all, so after our first leave we left Alan at home at the age of seven, just as we said we would never do. Even more cruelly we took the girls back to Assam, thus excluding him totally. He went to prep school, to what he later described as the worst experience of his life. When he got chickenpox and was sick his housemaster made him eat it as a punishment for making a mess. This, of course, we only learnt later. It was a famous school and we thought we were doing the best thing possible for him.

I was considered very eccentric for keeping the girls out in India till they were ten and eight, but the two years when I had them to myself and taught them by correspondence course were the happiest of my life in tea. They had ponies and goats as pets, they had a raft on the pond, and in the cold weather we did lessons outside under the rustle of bamboo leaves, with the rubber trees full of scarlet and gold minivets like candles. They had a Khasi ayah, unaccountably called Mrs. Dykes, who told them stories as she wandered through the tea bushes with them and the goats. Assam's plants, animals, birds and butterflies were an unending source of enrichment. Now I wonder why I sent any of the children home. I simply wasn't strong enough to hold out against the indoctrination of years, of a couple of centuries, of Indian lore. They were never consulted, any more than I had been.

So the wheel went irrevocably round, but now I was Out and they were at home being visited by a stranger at intervals. With air travel the intervals were shorter than they had been for me, and at least the three of them were together for holidays in a house in the Lake District which we had bought for our retirement, and in which my parents presently lived. But every time I flew over Europe and the jagged mountains of Arabia and the hot green sea of what was then Persia, and landed in the warm spicy air of India, I felt a traitor. I should never have let this happen again. Potten End, Aunt Margery, the flat dull days of Suffolk, the loss, the lack should have taught me.

*

In 1954 I left them all at home, and returned to Assam, sterilised, thirty two years old; to do what? Up till then the steaming, pulsating river valley had been a background for the children's needs. Now it had to fill mine or I would go mad. It was so beautiful and so full of interest that I must consider myself lucky. Indeed I did a lot of the time. We had moved to our last permanent garden which backed onto the Naga hills, down from which every morning flew those electric arcs of parrots which Poor Aileen had seen. Now I must notice them, even with sweat dripping from my forehead and the eyeflies stinging my lids.

March was when the eyeflies started, and we began our anti-malarial tablets. Ticks appeared on the dogs' ears and hibiscus flowers on the bushes and in April the tea bushes burst into precious leaf and girls danced in spring festivals with orchids behind their ears. The fan started to creak and warm brown water flowed from the taps, and in May a bird began to call, "You're ill, you're ill", and another, "Make more Pekoe" on a range of four notes.

May was mosquitoes and mini-cyclones which sent the shade trees crashing onto the newly sprouting tea bushes. May was cassias and laburnums standing like gold and scarlet umbrellas around us, and butterflies the size of birds, peppermint green and primrose yellow. May was legs bleeding from leech bites, and the throb of drums from the labour lines under enormous moons. May was moonflowers, opening huge and waxy white as you watched and filling the night with perfume.

In June purple clouds massed every day, thunder rumbled, and at last came wind and the driving wall of wetness; the gleam and gush of the south west monsoon, the smell of hot earth moistened, the glassy flap of rubber leaves. Roofs dripped, rivers gushed, frogs croaked and the temperature dropped a blessed ten degrees after downpours. In the flooded fields, pale green rice seedlings bent over their own shadows, and women moved like swans through the green sea of tea, plucking and plucking.

In spite of the rain it was steamily hot for three months. Mornings were spent under the verandah fan, afternoons having a siesta under the one in the bedroom. At five it was cool enough to go out for a walk through the tea bushes, and return to a tepid bath before the splendid setting of the sun at seven. Then the humming, squeaking, crackling, hooting night began, lit by fireflies and those enormous moons. We had to stay indoors behind our netted windows though, and went to bed early because there were few books to read and the wireless produced a lot of crackles and faint foreign voices. Even when deep freezes were invented we had none in our bungalows, though we eventually got air-conditioning. Nor did we have swimming pools, an extraordinary omission. Sometimes I dream I am back in Assam and the hot weather is just beginning, and my relief on waking is exquisite.

Tea garden

140

Then early in October there was a new smell and we walked out into a thick white mist and knew that the cold weather had begun; golden days when the compound filled with English flowers mixed in with mimosa and poinsettias, and the vegetable garden gave us salads and pineapples. The evenings were cool enough for fires and we played at being "home" with buttered toast in front of them. At weekends we went for fishing trips up the local river, and while Mac cast for mahseer I sat on sandbanks and cooked pots of rice over split bamboos which the boatmen collected. Kingfishers dropped into the water, fishing eagles soared, the brilliant banks of jungle were filled with monkeys, deer and clouds of butterflies. Sometimes the hillmen, the Nagas, would join us by our fire, shiny brown knees drawn up under their chins, laughing a lot to expose black teeth. We couldn't of course communicate with them, even in Assamese which many of them knew.

In the Autumn the tea was pruned and manufacturing stopped, so there was a lot of free time for managers and their assistants, and this was filled with Sprees. These were day long celebrations arranged by each club in turn, and were all exactly the same. The same teams played each other at polo, trestle tables supported the same salads, chicken and ham, soufflés and trifles; our cooks sweated over similar cakes for tea and wrote over them in green icing messages like Happy Xmas, Heep Heep Hurrah, Best Luck Sirs. In the evening the club was converted, with palm fronds and crepe paper, into whatever the club committee had decided was to be the motif for the year. It was really a waste of time, since everyone was exhaustedly drunk within the hour. A really successful Spree was one where the potted palms were used as goal posts and someone lost his trousers in a scrum down.

For years I considered it my wifely duty to trail through dust clouds to such torments of tedium through the cold weather. I could neither play games nor dance well so contributed nothing but my wilting presence, my tight dusty forehead, my eyes sunk into their sockets with strain and boredom, my throat dry and aching with the effort of suppressing yawns. If there is a God and he wants to think up a really good hell for me, he will send me on an eternal Assamese Spree.

Mac enjoyed it because he was good at all games, and liked to meet distant friends and discuss their shared world of plucking and drying and prices. As women, our conversation was limited to the even more constricted one of bungalow and compound. There was no bridge as had brightened the clubs of Mandalay and Rawal Pindi, no books to talk about. If anyone was enterprising enough to produce a scandal, we set on it like vultures, tearing out of it every last juicy thread of shocking surmise.

I sat down and thought seriously about all this when I returned to Assam without the children, and planned to do with my time what I had wanted since the days of scribbling plays in the Alps and sticking them into my knicker linings: write books. I drew my cane chair up to the verandah table each morning and under the squeak of the fan began a novel about a bored tea planter's wife whose children were at home. Graham Greene could have made such a tedious subject readable; my only resource was to have all the boring planters murder each other but even that didn't make the book interesting enough to sell.

When I raised my eyes from my typewriter to look around for something else to do, I couldn't believe I had been so blind. Weekly I had driven to the club through villages I had never entered, past people whose language I couldn't speak, living lives I knew nothing of, dancing and singing to unknown tunes. I had not, honestly, thought of them as people; they were a brownish blur, like the greenish blurs of the rice and the bluish ones of the mountains. They were categorised by planters as lazy, effeminate - the men tended to walk hand in hand - and spineless. Many of the women were very beautiful but would not be lured into white men's beds. They had to go to the carefree Khasis for their mistresses.

My heart thudded with excitement as I unwrapped Assamese grammars and awaited the schoolmaster Mac had ordered to come up to the bungalow and teach me. The first dry seed was being watered and I knew it would sprout into a profusion of bright flowers, through which I would step into a country neither my mother or grandmother or great grandmother had visited. At the time I didn't think in such terms, more as if I was being given the key of a cage. Learning the language would unlock me from the prison I had begun to recognise.

The schoolmaster's knees knocked together like castanets and he pulled his finger joints, crack, crack, crack, in an agony of embarrassment at sitting on the verandah of the Burra bungalow with the Burra Memsahib. It must have been a bit like being asked to Buckingham Palace to teach the Queen to type, so distant we were in our enormous bungalow on a hill from the tiny tin-roofed hut in which lived the assistant headmaster of the local school. He brought with him a book of etiquette, which, when I could read it, I discovered to be full of instructions about which hand to use for shaking and how to blow one's nose into a piece of cloth and put it into one's pocket; a revolting idea to Indians, but white men did it.

I never considered his ordeal, I used him as I used all other lowly employees around the place. He refused money and instead took to bringing me gigantic fish, as if I was doing him a favour in letting him spend his time on my verandah. When I tried to refuse the fish his eyes filled with tears and his knees knocked so violently that I feared for his bones. Mac said the fish was some sort of bribe, sooner or later one of the schoolmaster's sons would be asking for a job in his office, along with all the other Read-up-to-Class-Tens in the country. The fish would be unmentioned, but there in the background, great glistening reminders of past favours.

Several times he asked me to his house for a meal, which I ate alone in a room swept and cleaned and decorated with flowers. As I chewed my way through plates of curry and sweetmeats I heard the faint scuffling of his children next door, and wondered if they would have to go hungry as a result of my visit. His salary was half what I paid my cook, and he supported an old mother as well, who sat in a deck chair at the back of the house shooing the chickens off the drying grain. Part of their poverty was due to a debt incurred by his grandfather to a money lender, which had increased so much with compound interest that he said if he had another four sons they would never pay it off.

When we reached impasses of misunderstanding in the language, my teacher's teeth clashed as well as his knees. "Keethankeen," he said from between his chattering teeth. What? "Keethankeen," he pleaded, his jaw practically locking with frustration, until a long detour by way of brothers, sisters and mothers-in-law made it clear: kith and kin. We were neither of us helped by the grammar books, which were printed upside down and back to front by the Catholic Church's press. Yet I plodded through them very happily and spent evenings practising the new script, and the seed sprouted and sprouted.

I had no sooner mastered the present tense, than I was anxious to move out into the world that spoke this language. Tea estates ran schools jointly with the Government, and I thought I could kill several birds with one stone if I offered my services to our garden school. The headmaster said he would be greatly honoured to add me to his staff as long as I didn't expect to be paid, and showed me round. The school consisted of several rooms under a tin roof, provided with blackboards and desks. There was a large, new empty building next door, the Arts and Crafts Centre. Unfortunately it couldn't be used because there was no money for a teacher, but it raised the status of the school just by being there, and with it the salaries of the staff.

Starry-eyed, I saw my role at once, unpaid Art Mistress. Next morning I loaded the back of the Landrover with enormous lumps of clay, dug up by the malis and wrapped in wet cloth, and told the children who were lined up outside the school as a sort of guard of honour, that we would make fruit. I gave them each a piece of clay and they looked at it politely, their hands in their laps. "Like this," I said, and turned my lump into a banana. Obediently they turned their thirty lumps into bananas too. "Very educational," said the headmaster when he came to visit us, staring at a tableful of grey phallic symbols.

Next day I took down paint, and the bananas became more recognisable. I gave them more clay and asked them to make anything they liked. Without hesitation they embarked on more bananas. "Try them with bamboo, they know what to do with that," Mac suggested when I emptied a sackful of poison yellow phalluses onto the verandah at lunchtime. The bamboo produced bows and arrows from the boys, which they enjoyed shooting through the open windows, but the headmaster, who narrowly avoided having his ear pierced, said that though such extra-curricular activities were most character-forming, would I teach English instead?

So for the rest of the term, and several more, I stood under the tin roof with the heat beating down on my head, and taught Grammar and Composition and Macbeth. The children were mostly sons and daughters of the tea garden staff, a few of rich villagers. Labourers' children were needed around the house to look after their younger siblings, and then employed on the tea garden in simple, unskilled ways. New legislation after partition laid down rules about crèches and schools, but it was the studied aim of company boards to evade these as far as possible. If they built a crèche, it was a concrete room, unfurnished and uncarpeted, which could double as a cattle pound. The women preferred to take their children out into the tea, strapped to their backs or playing near. As for well equipped schools, what was the point, since there would be no jobs available. "Too many damned Bona Fide flunked B.A's around the place already," declared managers. Jo Coolie just needed his bowl of rice and his odd binge on local booze to keep him happy.

So I had on the benches in front of me beautiful golden-skinned girls with oiled plaits and gold ornaments, and equally beautiful boys in shirts and cotton trousers, all of whom seemed to be related to one another. "My auntie," a boy at the back announced proudly when I praised the work of the girl next to him. Some of the boys seemed about thirty, but all of them were keen and docile. Untrained, I made up in enthusiasm for the gaps in my skills. We played a lot of games and I took in pictures of Scotland to make blasted heaths recognisable.

The best boy in the class wrote all the essays, but the word cheat meant nothing to them. I complained to the headmaster and he wrote a model essay on the set subject and they all copied that. "But how can they learn?" I demanded crossly, and he lolled his head from side to side and wondered how indeed? This was a too backward country. Since all the girls would get married, and the boys find themselves lucky to get even menial jobs, he didn't think it mattered too much.

Sports days and prize-givings called for marquees and microphones and an agenda of twenty items. Speech-making was the passion of the Assamese, and though the microphone seldom worked, old men with long beards and few teeth hung onto it for twenty minutes of impassioned oratory. Their audience talked and went for walks, and I chewed aniseed and sweated until the last one had been finally prised from the microphone. Once there was a splendid public meeting called for a visit by the Minister of Education. It was dark when the National Anthem was finally sung and we tottered out into the teeming night. Then we found his car had broken down, and he and I sat by the side of the road together waiting for a tyre. "In a nut we are stranded," he declared calmly, as of a daily occurrence. We talked about Hegel and how Assam was in a state of transition, the excuse for all its difficulties. My forehead was caked with dust and sweat, my mouth full of the taste of aniseed, which I disliked, but up and up the shoots were growing.

My students started to ask me to their homes, to attend weddings or celebrate first menstruation, a big occasion in Assam. Brides with white flowers painted on their cheeks howled all through the ceremonies, the proper way to behave. The sprinkling of rice, the dancing round oil lamps, the playful wailing of the attendants delighted me. Villages were set in plantations of coconut and areka palms, usually round a pond on which ducks swam and water lilies lolled. I returned from my outings with my head swollen as in the days of my holy pleasure over curates.

"But the school is terrible," I told Mac. "No equipment, no text books." "They're bloody lucky to have a school at all," he said. I wasn't to ask him to dish out more money, because it simply wasn't there. The board at home wasn't interested, they felt it was the business of the government, and he agreed with them. Half educated youths in tight trousers were the scourge of the country, they should go out and get their hands dirty growing things in the fields. "What fields?" I shouted. "The tea companies have taken all the land from the people, there's no land left." "Balls!" he bellowed. "They're just too lazy to use it." These exchanges made us like strangers to one another, and I think Mac wished I was an ordinary wife, content with coffee parties. Nevertheless, he helped where he could, and was more sympathetic than he sometimes sounded.

I dreamt of a model school in Nazira, which was the administrative centre of the company's gardens. I filled it with airy classrooms, a laboratory, craft rooms provided with teachers. I brought out to it keen young men and women from England doing voluntary service, and I saw the Minister of Education's astonishment, and at his behest the instant transformation of all the schools of Assam. The bird in the hot nights no longer called "Make more pekoe" but "Beautiful schoo-hool". Mac said, "Darling, you're letting your imagination run away with you, that bird is indoctrinated by the board, it can't change any more than they can become interested in the education of Assam. All they are concerned with are their profits, as you know."

My crusading spirit increased with the amount of indifference it met. In the cold weather the chairman and a director or two made it their practice to pass the winter on a slow cruise at company expense, to visit their tea estates. They were doing us a great favour, leaving the frost and slush of their landed estates to sit about on our verandahs sipping the wine we had ordered up specially from Calcutta, bathed the while in warm sunshine and the smell of mimosa. The chairman told us that it took a toll of his dicky ticker, this first-class trip through the Mediterranean and the Indian Ocean and the onerous programme of chauffeur-driven tours from one lunch table to the next.

The chairman was a knight of the shires and a sitting member for somewhere or other, and a sitting target for my campaign. He had no sooner got himself settled in his cane chair with his iced gin in his hand, and told me he must compliment me, dear lady, on my splendid compound, how he rejoiced when his womenfolk busied themselves in useful ways, than I told him how this particular woman wanted to busy herself. I had drawn up a plan of the school for his inspection, but he peered at it under drooping lids, and said alas he had left his glasses in his room and in any case the times were such that schemes of this kind were pie in the proverbial sky.

He doubted, he doubted very much if times would ever improve sufficiently for his board to consider setting themselves up as a charity. He mumbled about swingeing post-partition taxes, and shed a rheumy tear or two into his gin about the days that were sadly departed and his disappointment in not being able to help me. He then returned to the topic that was engrossing him, his plans to "break" his son-in-law. I can't remember why he wanted to do this but it was a project to which he applied the little energy he had. Even his second concern, the clearing out of the "dead wood" from his plantations in the shape of inefficient managers, was marginal. I thought at first he was referring to shade trees, but Mac said he wouldn't know a shade tree from a coconut palm. He thought that if I produced too many maps of model schools he himself would come under this category.

So I put them away until the next director came out a month later. This time Mac was called away after dinner to some problem in the factory, and I had him to myself. But in no time he was too drunk to see my maps and told me instead about his problems with his mother, which caused him to choke. I had to thump him smartly on the back, and both his mother and model schools were forgotten for the rest of the evening as he continued to spit out bits of chicken, complaining huskily about this damn country, which only duty and his desire to get away from home induced him to visit.

So that was that, but I still had hopes of the immensely rich contractors who provided baskets, boxes, rice, petrol and gold coins at Christmas. I didn't mention this idea, but turned it over happily on my walks with the dogs through the pruned tea bushes. The school would bear the name of the donor, and a splendid opening ceremony would bring down the Chief Minister from Shillong, to stand in front of the flagging microphone and tell us of his pride in such a superb adornment to the Assamese scene. I would know enough Assamese by then to be able to answer him, to uproarious applause.

Before I had even drawn up a list of likely subscribers, Mac came home one lunchtime with a letter adorned with hearts and bright blue tear drops. It was in Assamese and I could decipher some of it. It was a passionate declaration of love, and it had caused uproar amongst the staff because it was sent to one of their daughters by a boy who was ten degrees below any category to be considered as a son-in-law. Moreover, he had gone to an arranged tryst with the girl carrying THREE UMBRELLAS.

The boy's refusal to explain the presence of the umbrellas was the last straw. With one voice the staff demanded that he be expelled from the school he attended with the girl. He was a snake in their grasses; who knew what other enormities he might commit, with or without umbrellas? None of their daughters would be safe for an instant. Meetings were held, microphones erected, resolutions passed. We laughed about it, and nearly split our sides when the boy was finally persuaded to reveal the role of the umbrellas. Why had he taken them that fatal evening? Well, because it was damn wet.

I stopped laughing when I discovered the boy was one of my best pupils about to matriculate. If he went, I went, I declared haughtily; and nobody argued. It was one thing to waste their time with clay bananas, it was quite another to interfere in social spheres beyond my understanding. Mac took the side of his staff and talked of wheels within wheels and there being more than met the eye in these things, it was a question of "izzat", reputation or self-esteem. I told him nastily not to lecture me about the customs of the country, I at least had learnt the language and knew a lot more about Assam than he did. It was not a happy time, but luckily we went on leave soon after.

*

When we returned I was fresh and enthusiastic again, turning from education to medicine. I particularly wanted to become involved in Family Planning work, since over-population was obviously at the root of India's problems. Mac said it wasn't a problem on the tea gardens, the board liked nothing better than to see a teeming mass of people wanting to work for it. It was a perfect mechanism for keeping wages down. "The board," I snorted, "judging by the ones I've met, all they're interested in is their family problems." Mac begged me to keep them out of it. I could visit the hospital and talk to the mothers and if they and the doctor agreed, they could be sterilised. The chairman's dicky ticker needn't beat faster for it.

Tea estates were very proud of their hospitals, which they often quoted as an example to the rest of the country. Each garden had one, and there was a central hospital for difficult cases and operations. Each garden hospital was provided with a qualified Dr Babu, and a dispenser. There were no nurses, the family of the patient squatted by the bed with food and attention. The wards, one for men, one for women and children, consisted of close rows of string beds, and were full of flies. Sanitation was primitive, the dirty linen was washed by the dhobi in the river.

A European doctor headed the system, and visited once a week, but as he was ignorant of the language, complaints had to be filtered through the Dr Babu, who made what he could of the patient's moans in a language sometimes even he couldn't understand since few of them spoke Bengali. His salary was considerably less than that of young European assistants coming out from home with no qualifications of any kind. Nobody thought this strange. The head clerk, who did the garden accounts, the engineer who kept the machinery running in the factory and on which depended the company's profits, earned a quarter of the salary of twenty-year-olds who would have had difficulty in mending a bicycle puncture. Whiteness was all when it came to assessing worth, and also when providing accommodation. Europeans were allotted bungalows with four bedrooms, set in a couple of acres. The Assamese staff lived close together in little brick boxes with tin roofs.

The labour force, imported mostly from Bihar and Orissa, lived in mud shacks in squalid settlements called "the lines". They were, of course, too simple-minded to know how to handle electricity or sanitation, and there was one water tap between twenty houses. "A lot better than they'd get at home," declared the chairman and everyone else, though none of them could have put a finger on the map to show where was home to their fortunate labour force. In the early days of tea, recruiting officers had scoured the famine-haunted south for tea pluckers, since the local peasants had refused to leave their clean villages and huddle in slums round the factories. Breeding had done the rest, producing a happy state of over-population, and consequent rock-bottom wages.

My mission was to halt this process. The company cannily paid part of its labour force's wages in rations of rice and flour, so that to be unemployed was an extra burden; it was better to earn a pittance and get food at reduced rates. Of course, my grasp of what was going on came to me gradually as I moved into the system and opened eyes that had been looking elsewhere for fifteen years. I had walked past the "lines" with my dogs, and seen without seeing the leaking hovels with open drains round them, the thin cows tethered to keep them out of the tea where my herd gorged, the children with matchstick legs flopping in the mud. Occasionally I marvelled that my servants could emerge from such surroundings and become the crisp, efficient bearers of trays round my polished rooms. It never seemed my business to enquire about their families, nor to wonder what they felt handing round the six course meals at my dinner parties, they, who lived on one meal of rice and lentils a day. I still - and I blush to admit it - thought of them as in some way inferior, and happy with their ignorant lot.

But now, as I sat on the string beds with the women, whose blood was often the colour of honey, and waved the flies off the faces of their minuscule pink-palmed babies, I was glum with guilt. Their expectations might not be high, but they deserved better than this. Mac was sympathetic, but constrained by what he was allowed to allot out of garden funds. He installed fly-proof doors in the hospital, but couldn't tackle the much more urgent needs for sanitation and plumbing in the lines. The winter visits of the directors and their wives, if forgone, would just about have paid for this, but this argument wouldn't have weighed heavily in discussions at board level.

A much better argument, a perfectly obvious truth it seemed to me, was that the improved health of the work force would save the enormous amount spent on drugs, which was always being cited as proof of the splendid care the Company took of its people. Why did the women's blood come out yellowish-pink when it was tested after childbirth, so that they had to be pumped with iron and vitamins? Because their husbands drank away their wages, said most planters, if they thought about the subject. God, compared to the rest of the country they were bloody lucky. I had heard about this incredible luck of tea garden labourers for years, and accepted it as truth. The rest of India was always out there as a comparison.

Work on a tea estate was frequently compared to a piece of cake by planters who drove through the bushes in their land-rovers. I too had watched the women, stiff and elegant as they bent and stretched above the glossy leaves, and thought what a peaceful way it was to earn a living. From dawn to dusk they plucked and threw the leaves into baskets and then carried the heavy load to a central point, leaving their babies on the grass to be watched by older children. Twice they would be brought tea in kerosene tins, and at the end of the day they would snake in pretty white columns back to the factory, for a final tally.

For the men the work was less arduous, their hands were not as agile as a woman's and they were put to other tasks: weeding, spraying, manuring. They also worked in the factory, in an inferno of heat and dust. At any hour of the day or night the hooter would call them to shovel the withered leaf in and out of roaring ovens. The noise was deafening, and the torrid air full of particles of tea. How this affected their lungs nobody ever enquired. A woman's job in the factory was to squat and sort the fired leaf into piles, easy work and even more badly paid.

Until I touched and talked to the mothers in the hospital, I never considered the women anything more than a composite entity: The Women. I didn't know what they ate, how many children they had, their life expectancy, their hopes and dreams if any. All the bungalow servants were men, and the only time women came within close range was when Mac sent teams of rather elderly ones to pull up the weeds on the lawn. I sat on my verandah and watched them shuffle along on their heels and thought they looked like penguins, bless them. It never occurred to me to wonder if my grandmother would have enjoyed spending her declining years wrenching at sharp grasses under a blazing sun.

Central to my stupidity over the years was my acceptance of other people's standards, even people I didn't particularly respect. Plantations made their profits from the exploitation of cheap labour, and you can't exploit without degrading. Yet this simple equation had eluded me, and it wasn't until I moved close, physically close, to the women in the hospital that it became blindingly obvious. I knew there was little I could do to raise the standard of their pay or conditions, but at least I could stop them ruining their health with endless pregnancies, and producing children for whom there would be no work and no future. The trouble was, I found, to persuade them to believe my saving message. Though many of them agreed, their mothers-in-law forbade them to limit their families, and their husbands were suspicious. There was also the fear of going for sterilisation to the central hospital, which in their minds was connected with terminal illness and death.

The only way to convince them was to call a public meeting to be addressed by the Minister of Health through several microphones. I wrote off to Shillong asking for this minister, but was sent instead the head of Family Planning for the state, a Miss Sing. She arrived with a suitcase full of contraceptives which she unpacked on arrival and laid out on the verandah table, much to the embarrassment of Mac and Father James, the Catholic priest who was unfortunately our other weekend guest. He often came to stay, a delightful man whose little flock were the most anaemic of all the work force, since he forbade them the alcohol that might have provided a few calories.

Miss Sing was newly appointed to her job, and bursting with enthusiasm. As she explained over dinner, her first task was to discover the sexual habits of the people. She had prepared questionnaires which, when filled in, would solve the mystery in minutes. Mac said nobody would be able to read them, let alone fill them in, and

Father James shrugged his shoulders and said the wombs of his converts were in the care of the good Lord.

But your good lord is over-generous isn't it, shrieked Miss Sing. How is it he makes them so sexually active, these poor people? How can he allow them to have intercourse every night and thus produce more children than they or the country could support? Mac said it was about the only fun they had and it wasn't fair to deprive them of it. Who is talking of depriving? Miss Sing wanted to know. As a single woman she had to take the pleasures of sex on hearsay of course, and she laughed loud and girlishly about this, but all she was asking of them was to use one or other of her contraceptives.

Later, when she had gathered up her rubber objects so that the bearer could put down the coffee tray, we asked Father James to sing. He had once been training for opera, and his beautiful voice drowned the night sounds, and also the voice of Miss Sing, till bed-time. Mac and I laughed a lot about the evening when at last it was over, but he was not optimistic about the questionnaires which he said would be used to light fires, and he foresaw the air being full of little flying rubber saucers projected from catapults. He could bet his bottom dollar that one thing they would never do with dutch caps was to wear them.

Mac ordered all the women to attend the meeting next morning, and they sat in polite rows in front of Miss Sing while she explained in vague and delicate language the use of the rubber objects on the table in front of her. Then I got up and told them I had been sterilised and that was why I only had three children and could run a car and eat three meals a day. Some children danced and then the microphone was taken over by the usual gang of old men, the while Miss Sing distributed her questionnaires. In a last fiery speech she exhorted them to remember that their country depended on them not producing too many children. "Jai Hind!" they all cried obediently, and filed out to the strains of Auld Lang Syne supplied by the head clerk's ancient gramophone.

I was available every morning at the hospital to hand out condoms and caps, but nobody came to claim them. Not a single questionnaire was filled in. For Christ's sake, said Mac, they wouldn't know what intercourse meant, and even if they did would they be likely to write down how often they had it, even if they could remember? That wasn't important, I argued, but surely some of them would want to limit their families? Two women, in fact, came forward to be sterilised, and I persuaded my cook and dhobi to have vasectomies, and that was the extent of my great plan to put India right. Mac tried to be sympathetic, but couldn't conceal his relief that he wouldn't have to spend another evening with Miss Sing.

I continued to visit the hospital because it was the door through which I could enter the women's lives. I needed them more than they needed me, and I particularly needed one little girl who lay alone in a bare room, wasting away with TB. Since she was infectious nobody went near her, and she lay with her bony arms on the coverlet, staring at the walls, uncomplaining and listless. What a way to help her to recovery, I exclaimed, and hurried down daily with armfuls of paper and crayons, beads for threading, books and a beautiful dressed doll I had kept in a cupboard since the children left.

I brushed the child's matted hair and tied ribbons in it, and she began to smile when she saw me, her dull eyes faintly animated. She particularly liked the doll. She held it in her thin arms all the time, and the Dr Babu said she talked to it when I had gone. She couldn't talk to me because she spoke a dialect I didn't know, but familiarity flowed between us; I thought love. "Her condition is transforming itself," the Dr Babu assured me.

One morning her bed was empty. Her family had taken her home, along with the books and beads and the beautiful doll. She was so much improved that the Dr Babu felt this a safe move. A few weeks later when I asked how she was he told me she had died. I went home and threw myself on my bed and beat my head against the pillow, convinced that I had killed her with my presents, that her family had coveted the beautiful doll more than the sick child. Mac said nonsense, she was incurable and at least I had cheered her for a month or two. "Oh this country," I howled, turning against India as we all did when things went wrong.

Iris in Assam

After our next leave Fiona and Anne came out with me, and I was occupied for two years with five O-levels with Anne. Fiona was sixteen, the age I had been when I was brought Out, but instead of casting around for a husband for her, I dreaded the thought that one of her dancing partners should turn out to be the man of her dreams. Only a financial crisis had persuaded me to have her out, and I hoped that it would just be a stop-gap between school and Art College; and so it turned out. At

151

last the spell was broken; no more Jones women would sit beneath their fans mourning for the children they had sent away.

When we returned alone after our next leave, it was our last "tour" before retirement. At forty one I felt old and wise. Though some of the seeds had sprouted and then withered prematurely, I felt there were others that even at this late stage might flower. I knew with absolute certainty how I didn't want to spend my time: at the club, at coffee parties, at Sprees. I made friends with an Assamese family and with their help collected folk tales and translated them, and wrote an article which was accepted by "History Today". I walked through the tea with beating heart and burning cheeks, chewing the bitter leaf buds, assured that this was the beginning of a literary career. With the money I made from a best-seller, I could tell the chairman what to do with his dicky ticker, and his purse strings, and build my model school unaided. I would walk through its airy classrooms, a mixture of Florence Nightingale and Joan of Arc, adored by all.

My daydreaming was interrupted that winter by the unexpected appearance of the Chinese army in Assam. As the humming birds clinked in the mimosa, our radios told us that this army was pouring down towards the tea gardens of Assam. Nehru broadcast to the nation of how his heart was bleeding for the people of that far province. At polo matches, on the rare occasions that I attended them, I found the women knitting balaclavas for the soldiers who, we heard, were being sent up into the Himalayas in cotton shirts and sandals.

One evening the mailbag contained an order for the women (the European women) to leave. We were to meet at a collecting point, wearing strong comfortable shoes in case we had to walk to Calcutta, and carrying enough food for the journey. I protested that I wanted to stay, but Mac said I would be a terrible worry to him and anyway orders were orders. Sulkily, miserably, I collected four dozen hard boiled eggs and some photographs in a paper bag, and allowed myself to be driven through cheering, laughing Assamese villagers, who found this Flight of the White Women the best entertainment for years. No thought had been given for the protection of their wives and daughters should the Chinese arrive to rape them. As their laughing faces disappeared into the dust behind us, I wondered if perhaps they might even welcome the Chinese as an improvement on haughty, uncaring us.

In the event, we didn't have to walk, some Hastings bombers came to fly us out, being company wives and the wives of rich contractors, whose arms dangled over the edges of their seats solid with gold bracelets; presumably their husbands had paid large sums to the RAF or the company or both for the privilege denied to anyone else Indian, but poor. The seats of the plane were back to front, which added to the unreality of the experience. This was my second retreat from an enemy; first the Japanese, now the Chinese, finally it would be Pakistan. The flight Maria made over the river to Loodeanah in the Mutiny was probably more frightening, but her over-riding sensation likely to have been the same: disbelief.

It was a creased and dispirited band who crossed the tarmac in their sensible shoes when we finally landed at Dum Dum airport. We had spent a night at our collecting point, a local clubhouse, our hard boiled eggs between our knees and nowhere to lay our heads. One or two sensible souls had replaced the eggs with bottles of gin, and were happily insensible when it came to embarkation, but most of us brooded soberly on our fate should the Chinese make a sudden spurt and arrive to find us all conveniently collected in one place.

Outside the airport building, benches and trestle tables had been set up, on which were placed freshly cut sandwiches. These were handed to us by ladies in starched seersucker outfits, whose laundered look made us even more conscious of our creases. "You are DP?" said a man with a list, waiting to tick me off. Yes I was a displaced person, I said; or perhaps he was describing me as a damaged parcel. The sudden Indian night fell on us as one by one we were collected by limousine and driven off.

I found myself, with two other women and their children, in an enormous marble-floored mansion, such as abounded in Calcutta amongst the filthy shacks and the huddled bodies of the sleeping homeless. It was owned by one of the company's contractors, who let it out as a Chummery, a hostel for bachelors. Fortunately all the resident chums were away on leave, and so we had the use of its vast glistening rooms, and were waited on by its countless servants. It was good to hand over our eggs, and to wash off two days' dirt in a marble bath. The whole place seemed to have been hacked out of solid seams of white marble.

Nobody knew why the Chinese had arrived in Assam, so there was no telling if and when they would leave. The wireless produced distant cricket matches, but no word of our invaded state. Company agents visited us and asked if we were comfortable and said they would tell us what the chairman and board had decided to do with us. As the days passed and they got no directives from home they became tetchy and muttered about returning chums who would need their rooms. I thought the chairman was probably on his way out to visit us, blissfully unaware of the news. I felt immensely in love with India, I didn't want to be flown home as some of the women were. In its hour of need surely it needed me?

I decided to try and get a job, and live in a YWCA hostel. I went to a refresher course in shorthand, where a little man in a plum coloured sweater called Sir reminded me of how to write "at the discretion of the chief engineer" in one squiggle. "Oh Sir," we panted, "Not so fast Sir." A very old lady sitting next to me said there was no chance of us getting jobs at our age, however good our shorthand. As I stood in the gutter waiting to pick up a taxi, a man with a long shiny car and a foreign accent tried to pick me up. Here I am, I thought, a loiterer in a sleazy street, unwanted, unemployable, homeless. And yet at the same time there was this great irrational love for India, stronger than I had ever felt it in my comfortable hours.

Blood was needed for the wounded in the Himalayas, so next day one of my friends in the chummery went with me to donate ours. I had a heavy cold, but this wouldn't affect my blood, and a great deal of arm-prodding managed to convey to the taxi driver where we wanted to go. He drove as all taxi drivers in Calcutta, very fast with his hand on the horn and his head out of the window shouting obscenities at other drivers, but got us eventually to the blood donor centre. It was locked. We picked our way over piles of wood to the back door, but it looked as if it had been shut for weeks. We went to the cinema to cheer ourselves, and the newsreels were all of the wicked invaders of India's north-eastern passes. When the lights went on, the audience turned out to be entirely composed of Chinese, filling in their time as they had closed and barred their shoe shops against possible reprisals.

As nobody wanted my shorthand or my blood, I sent off an advertisement to the local paper to say I would give English lessons in return for a room. I waited in to take all the phone calls that would result, but nobody wanted my English either. Waking each morning to the cawing of crows and the roar of traffic, I longed for the mist rising from my Assam garden, with the egrets standing hunch-backed like fielders on a cricket pitch. I longed for the rainbow dew dripping off the mimosa, and the Naga hills resting beneath their clouds. The two women with me went off to swimming clubs and race meetings, making a happy best of the situation. As usual, I managed discontent without remedy. This, looking back, was my constant Indian mood.

And then suddenly, on the day our tickets home were to be delivered, we heard that it was over, the Chinese were on their way out of Assam and we were free to go back. I bought two green parrots from a man selling them on the pavement, and let them loose. They shot up into the sky in wild delight, and I knew exactly how they felt. On my way back an hour later, two more parrots had taken their place on the man's arm; or perhaps the same ones, trained to return. Who was I fooling when I thought I could rescue even a pair of birds?

Would I go back and try to fight everything? The chairman, the educational system, the club committee, everyone's idea of my role in the community? Or would I, could I, live easily, contentedly, acceptingly, like the other wives? I stood in the Calcutta street and felt that I had choices, but knew in my heart that somewhere in my genes or experience I was programmed. I had to feel in a certain way, and then act on feelings.

I flew back a couple of days later. Assam was quiet and green and oh so beautiful, the rice crop being cut which we had feared would go to feed the Chinese army. The cook was waiting at the bungalow, cracking his knuckles in the same irritating way, wearing the woolen cap through which I suspected he strained the soup; and the dogs, and Miranda the deer; and Mac, and the mimosa and parrots and cloud muffled hills. I swore I would never take any of them for granted again. I would fight less and love more. I would preserve and cherish this mood of delirious relief.

*

So I was receptive to an invitation, a couple of weeks later, from my Assamese friends, to visit a holy island on the Brahmaputra, inhabited entirely by monks. I visualised leafy hermitages such as those described in the Ramayana, and very enlightened old men with long white beards waiting with words of wisdom. There was to be a night-long drama on the life of Lord Krishna, a yearly event. It all sounded wonderful. Mac thought it might be a shambles; he listed the things that would probably go wrong: the Baruas would miss the boat; the boat would miss its moorings; the monks would get the date of the festival wrong; the drama company booked to perform would have gone to Afghanistan instead. I knew I was going to have a memorable experience and my receptive mood was not going to be affected by his warnings.

He sent me off with bedding, and provisions for a fortnight, adding the possibility of floods and earthquakes to the things that could go wrong on a long weekend. I was to wire him if I wanted a helicopter to pluck me up from amongst my monks, whom he suspected of being a chilarky lot of misfits who would want me to get them jobs with the company. I told him to stop talking like a typical planter. The young wife of our new scientific officer was coming with me, a girl fresh from university and still unaware of what she ought to be feeling and doing.

The rest of the party consisted of the Barua mother and daughter, and an aunt. When I went to collect them I found that they, too, were well provided, with several wicker baskets containing live chickens, rice and oranges. The aunt had also brought a large tin of cooking fat with which to anoint the sacred feet of a special monk. It was quite a job to maneuver both buxom ladies, their bedding and the baskets into the car. Luckily, Brenda was slim and carried only packet soups and a sleeping bag.

It took even greater skill to get us aboard the river steamer, on which we were to cross to our holy island. As we stood pinned to the side of the boat, hemmed in by about two thousand eager pilgrims bringing bicycles, I remembered how many times I had read of overcrowded boats sinking with the loss of all passengers. As soon as we started our slow progress into midstream, the aunt said she was going to vomit and very soon did, all over my shoes. Someone managed to find room to set up a kerosene stove and fry curry. The smell of spices and bicycle oil and a great many hot bodies made it all very festive, but I was glad to arrive. The Brahmaputra is like an inland sea, with the far banks out of sight.

We were met on the island by a cousin of the Baruas in his car, to drive us to our hostel. He was an extremely jovial man, much addicted to Wordsworth who seemed to have been on the curriculum of Assamese schools for many years, so many people quoted him. This cousin treated us to "Daffodils" and snatches of the "Immortality Ode" as he raced us along dirt roads through a landscape rather bare and flat. I presumed the monks were elsewhere. This was the world's largest river island, and stretched for miles. When he left us at the hostel, I remarked on how nice he was, but Anima the daughter shook her head and said he had no marriage prospects, he was too black.

While the chickens were being slaughtered and turned into curry, we sat on our grey mattresses in the hostel. Mrs Barua and the aunt prayed, Anima told us about the monks, who were members of a reformed branch of Hinduism that flourished in Assam. One of the monasteries had at its head a very special saintly man, and it was for his holy feet that the tin of Cocogem was intended. Anima herself found such practices old fashioned, but the older women liked to continue them. Brenda asked intelligent questions and we both scratched as the inmates of the mattresses came out of the flock for their evening meal.

Next day, driven by the poetic cousin, we went in search of this man, the aunt clutching the Cocogem which was beginning to melt in the heat. All the dusty red tracks we took led to the wrong sacred feet. We all began to melt, though only I grew fretful. Partly it was because the island was uniformly flat, cultivated, sprinkled with ordinary houses, though the driver insisted on comparing most of them to Wordsworth's cottage. It was not at all the enchanted forest I had foreseen, where silver deer might step out of the shadows and turn out to be Siva in disguise.

By midday Brenda and I were not only disappointed, but dehydrated. Perhaps the monastery had closed down, I suggested, as we lurched down one more side track leading to a village they didn't recognise. No, they were sure they would have heard, they said, calm and hopeful, and this irritated me even more. Typical, typical, the word hummed round in my head, along with Mac's warnings; typical were the overcrowded boat, the sick on my shoes, the grimy mattresses, the tough curry, the melting fat, the non-existent monk. Sweat ran into my eyes, which I closed, and tried to close my mind too. Just beneath the surface still lay layers of prejudice which I hated to have revealed.

"Ah, now we are here," said Mrs Barua, and I opened my eyes in surprise. We had reached a white, thatched building surrounded by a few dusty trees. A lame deer and a couple of cows were grazing the scant grass. We climbed out, our knees unfolding with a loud sucking sound, so glued they were with sweat, and mounted some steps onto a stone verandah. Here we sat on the ground with our backs to the wall, along with several other expectant pilgrims. For a long time nothing happened, and then a man appeared with a tray on which there were bowls of dry rice, and curds, and cups of water. The rice stuck to the top of my dry mouth, so I took the water. It looked cloudy, as if it had been used to wash the sacred feet, but I was terribly thirsty so I sipped a little. Nothing happened again, but only I felt impatient. I closed my eyes and breathed deeply, but across the dark screen of my mind flashed the word "typical" again. Would these people never learn how to organise?

When I opened them there was a man sitting cross-legged opposite us. He was plump and dressed in a simple white unstitched garment. He sat absolutely still, only his smile flowed from him, and across the stone, and over my knees like sunlight. Then his smile turned to laughter, shaking his shoulders, rippling down his arms into his upturned palms. Lifting his hands he spilt his laughter over us, pouring it in a solid and shining stream over our heads, down our backs, easing the heat and the strain and the tiredness, a benediction.

One by one we went forward to touch the holy feet. The aunt loosened her hair and with it rubbed in some of the fat from her tin. When she returned to her place beside me, her greasy hair about her shoulders, I asked if I could borrow the fat.

156

Nothing seemed more right than to anoint his feet with it, but as I approached he leant forward and put it aside. He didn't think it appropriate, it seemed, and what he thought I thought. Close to him was the peace that passes understanding, mothballs and sandalwood, and red and gold palaces.

I asked him to bless me, and in halting English he said we would bless each other. He held his open palms before me and said they were waiting for my troubles, wherever I was, whenever I needed them. Then he laid a hand on my head and said there was a great boulder between me and the wisdom I was seeking. Time and patience would shift it, and his prayers and mine. He said he hoped I would come back. If he only knew - perhaps he does - how often I have crossed that green river, and driven that long red road, and climbed those steps, and laid my aching head down at his sacred feet.

The cousin drove us to the drama that evening, a little drunk but still able to produce Gray's "Elegy" in more or less the right verse order. He had read up to Class Ten he said, and would my husband please find him a job in the tea garden? He would be prepared to live in a humble cot like Wordsworth's and would daily pray for me and the fruit of my loins. He whizzed erratically off, scattering hens and goats, and the aunt said that his family, connected to her husband, were all no good alcoholics. They were well provided with taxis, but short on brides which was only to be expected.

The drama, which started two hours later, was predictable, but in my mood I laughed at Krishna's pranks, at his more adult philanderings amongst milkmaids, at his creaking battles with monsters and violent jealous kings. I sat, like the rest of the audience, with a silly smile of approval on my face as the cardboard swords clashed, and dancers stamped round the ladders on which were perched electricians, trying for the fourth time to mend the lights. The sun was rising behind the bamboos when we finally left Lord Krishna still piping to his milkmaids and went in search of the driver. He was not to be found, but somebody else appeared to take us back to the hostel, exhausted, exhilarated, and in my case in some deep centre of my being, quite changed.

When I got back Mac said, well, had it been the typical chaos he had predicted. And I said, yes and no, and made a funny story of the poetical cousin and the electricians, but guarded the truth. The truth I suppose was that another seed had been watered, but I wanted these flowers to be sacred, like lotuses in the holy writings which I now devoured as fast as I could find them. Buddhist scriptures appealed to me most but all my reading told me the same thing; the boulder that he had said was blocking me from wisdom was the elusive, the transitory ego, that insisted on its own importance but stood in the way of understanding. Understanding was what the enlightened ones arrived at, who were like lamps in windless places. They did not flicker in any wind of disappointment. They did not rush hither and thither, driven by anger, hot, cold, hurt, frustrated.

I copied out texts and kept them in a cardboard box, to be taken like pills when I sagged. "He who regards pain and pleasure alike, who dwells in his own self, who looks upon a clod, a stone, a piece of gold as of equal worth, who remains the same amidst the pleasant and unpleasant things, who regards both blame and praise as one", he has wisdom. With the tiny chisel of faith I must chip away at the boulder, day by day, minute by minute.

I saw my efforts in schools and hospitals as patronising and ego-centred efforts to make myself feel good. No wonder nothing had worked, since the hub of every wheel was myself, the energy that turned it my desire to show off. Selflessly, selflessly I must simply see the next thing to do, and do it. The images proliferated: dew drops sliding into the sea; lotus leaves resting on ponds; candle flames steady where no wind could reach them.

When the chairman sat on my verandah and said how frightfully proud he was of his women-folk not losing their heads and flying home in the emergency, I smiled serenely. Chip, chip, I wouldn't gratify my foolish ego by pointing out that we had had no choice since he and the board had ignored the telexes that had flown home hourly about us. I would try not even to think such things, since in the mind lay all the causes that led to the foolish effects.

It was easy in the cold weather. Mac had accepted that I wasn't going to accompany him to polo matches and Sprees, and left me sitting on the verandah working on a children's book and reading Indian history, spurred on by several more "History Today" articles. The bitter, explosive novel on the world of tea planting was forgotten about; I had considered that it was the only kind I could write, but now it seemed that all the anger and frustration it would release could be dissipated calmly in meditation. Mac was constantly angry and frustrated too, because of a general manager who was abrasive, ruthless, insensitive and almost certainly dishonest. General managers, like the colonels of our regiment, were a job lot; not surprising when considering the board who chose them. Mac decided to ask for early retirement, voicing the view almost daily that he might commit murder if he had to endure another year of this maniac, and have to spend his declining years in Gauhati gaol making bamboo baskets.

So when the days grew warm, and the bird began to call "You're ill, you're ill", I ignored the rubber bands tightening round my gut, and the nausea and pain that meant another attack of amoebic dysentery. Most people had this on and off in Assam, and pills would usually cure it, but this time my symptoms grew so severe that I was sent up to Shillong to spend three weeks in hospital having an intensive course of treatment. I returned feeling as if I had been put through a mangle, but determined to enjoy everything about this last hot weather: the blue jays lying like gorgeous fans on the grass, their wings outspread; the morning and evening arcs of parrots; the monthly miracle of moonflowers. My barking deer Miranda, reared from a small orphan, I would cherish for this last few months before releasing her into the jungle, a distant one so that this time she wouldn't return.

Then one morning I found myself jumping aside as I passed an allamanda bush, terrified of touching one of its poisonous golden flowers. In case I had accidentally brushed against one, I hurried back to the bungalow to wash my hands. Who knew what else might poison me? My hands became white and bubbly from constant washing, and my beautiful garden turned into a deadly dangerous area through which I tiptoed, my arms clamped to my sides. Quite soon I didn't dare venture into it, and anyway grew too weak to walk further than faltering steps round the verandah, since food was certain to be contaminated and unsafe to eat. Mac got tranquillisers for me, but I flushed them down the lavatory.

THE END AND THE BEGINNING

There is some sort of symbolism in the fact that I, the last of the Jones girls, was carried home from India more or less prostrate. It was a punishment perhaps, because none of us had contributed much to the country that had given us livelihoods for so long. If I had been in a state to consider the matter at the time, I would have wept gallons of regretful tears on all our behalfs.

Maria's eighteen years were meager of any understanding or affection for Indians. Her horror of "colour" was passed on to her daughter, my grandmother, and then to her daughter, my mother. A brown skin was *de facto* disgusting. Indians, poor things, were brown, and as such inferior absolutely and beyond argument. My grandmother in Burma didn't despise so much as ignore. Burmans flitted about like pretty butterflies, part of the scenery and much to be admired in passing but not to be taken seriously; mixed marriages were more common, there was less revulsion felt for golden skins, though of course their possessors couldn't pass through the portals of the Club.

My mother's Indian years were devoted largely to enjoyment, which for her involved a lot of dogs to breed and show, bridge, tennis and parties. It was all very Kipling and most of it harmless. Extravagant and extrovert, she was living the kind of life that best suited her, and expressed never a qualm about its quality. She often alluded to being "desperately hard up" but this poverty sat lightly on her and didn't interfere with her social life. Her happy marriage didn't interfere with flirtations and affairs either. She, more than anyone I've known, could happily reconcile opposites. Her chameleon character allowed her to fit whatever role she was presently playing.

I took India a lot more seriously, and the nervous breakdown that ended my years there was the outcome. Body and mind had had enough, too much. I'd had too much amoebic dysentery, and too much treatment for it. I'd struggled too long and unsuccessfully to create what felt like a useful life, suited to my needs. I felt as if I'd been swimming against the current for year after hot and useless year, a lone swimmer what's more, neither waving nor drowning, just ineffectually thrashing about.

This is a retrospective appraisal. At the time, my sense of isolation was relieved by a house full of pets to be cherished, and a beautiful garden full of birds and butterflies and flowering shrubs and trees. In spite of spaces between us, there was also much of my marriage on the credit side. Mac gave me as much encouragement as his position and his own rather conservative instincts allowed. He always liked a conventional and routine existence - the army had made him very happy - and a planter's round of work, games and early to bed, suited him very well.

Why, I wonder, didn't it suit me? Most women liked it, none that I knew questioned why there had to be two worlds, us driving from our luxurious bungalows to our well appointed clubs, them living out there in their mud huts. None wanted to penetrate that other world to see if its inhabitants could be contacted. When I say none, I mean not one. So I stroked my barking deer and cuddled a series of little gibbons and didn't notice that my mind was growing like the inside of a golf ball, tightly wound rubber strands that finally snapped.

I never found the journal of a planter's wife in Assam to set beside my own experience, and I don't know if anyone else broke down there, apart from Poor Aileen. Up to the Second World War there were not a lot of women there, although one of them was Mac's aunt, Annie, but for some reason I never questioned her about her life on a tea estate in the twenties. In her freezing Edinburgh house there were a lot of tiger-skin rugs and the stories that went with them, but she didn't describe how she spent her time.

A lot of it, I suspect, in fretting for her children at home, and here is the irony of our Indian lives: we abandoned our children to others, causing misery all round, and for what? To occupy the place which society said we must, at our husbands' sides. Husbands Came First we were all told, and our duty was to remain with them in whatever dreary backwater they landed us. Many a moral story my mother told me of women who had left their men to spend a little time with their children, and found themselves displaced forthwith. "Of course she brought it on herself" was the punch-line of these yarns, ending with abandoned wives living on pittances in Crawley or Haslemere. The solution, to open schools in hill stations for English children, was abandoned after Minnie's time for reasons I've never quite understood. It could have been the number and variety of tropical illnesses to be guarded against. There also grew up a snobbish conviction that if you were educated in India that terrible tarbrush must have touched you.

For my grandmother and my mother, the pain of separation was alleviated by the pleasure they found in the Eastern scene, or rather in the view from the bungalow and club verandahs. I felt myself imprisoned on those verandahs a lot of the time, a matter of temperament I suspect, an influx from my father's side. One lot of his forebears settled near Calcutta as missionaries and became part of the scenery, a subject my mother avoided. Her Jones instincts alerted her to the dangers they must have run into of becoming "dhesi". I think their venturing outside the conventions must have been communicated to me in some eccentric gene. My mother thought so too.

It has taken a long time to read through all the diaries and letters, and with the help of my mother's memories, to piece together the story of four generations of a family and its connections with the East. The children were the sacrificial victims of Empire, all those pathetic little parcels sent home by P&O; but all the women and their wasted talents are to be pitied too. The Poor Aileens and Flos and Sheilas were victims, and if they faltered on the altar steps it was too bad. It was back to the albums, the dried flowers, the newspaper cuttings about those dizzy successes in Deal. It was into an asylum if they actually fell down and made a noise about it.

The beauty and brains with which they were endowed did little for them. Their role was second rate, and the very best they could aspire to was to be elegant hostesses for the advancement of their menfolk, be these brothers or husbands. When all is said and read, the Jones women emerge from the past as ciphers, doing simply what was expected of them in a ladylike way. Only the barneys and the scenes at breakfast belie their compliance. They were like miniature volcanoes, ready to erupt for the slightest reason, or no reason at all.

Their values were quaint, and only to be understood in context. They took them to India and Burma, the ones who went, wore them as a protection like solar topees and veils, against the threatening hordes of the brown, the pagan, the ignorant poor. Thus walled in, physically and mentally, they managed to reproduce Eastbourne and Leamington Spa all over the East, though never for a moment would they have thought of it as Home. The snarling tiger heads and Persian rugs festooned over their retirement homes showed a certain nostalgia for the India they had enjoyed: the "shikar" in the cold weather camps with elephants kneeling down to be mounted; the colourful bazaars where you could "beat down" the sellers of the polished stones and brass and exquisite carved ivory. Many a yarn was told over tiffin of the bazaar-wallahs wheedled into parting with precious ware for practically nothing.

It has been quite hard work, keeping up with the Joneses, feeling a mixture of pity and irritation, wondering why and at what point I came to discard their values. It was inevitable I think, but hardly sensible. My life in India was as unproductive as theirs, but a lot less comfortable. Cuckoo Cousin Mary and I take our eccentric way through the family story hand in hand, simply being the people we had to be.

Without the Indian connection there would have been less guilt, less feeling of a wasted opportunity. And yet in the end it is Burma that haunts me, the country I never visited. Some illogical insistence I carry round, that its red palaces were not destroyed by our armies; that round the bend of a great river there is a house in which my grandmother lives, surrounded by the smell of sandalwood. Because I loved her, I accepted her version of the truth about it. I long for a place that never existed, being the true daughter of my mother in not being able to separate truth from fantasy.

I call it imagination, and have used a lot of it in this story, whether wisely or extravagantly I'm not sure. It has been a journey of discovery, and like all worthwhile journeys there has been no particular point of arrival.

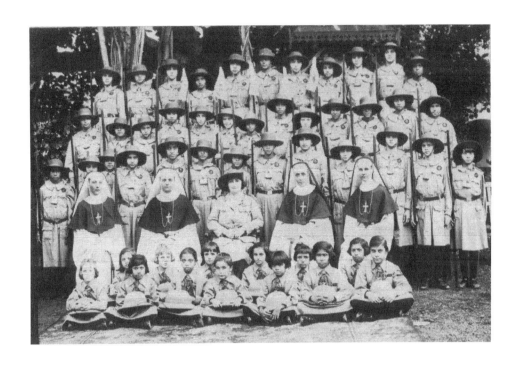

Iris Macfarlane was born in 1922 and married Donald Macfarlane in 1940. She spent more than twenty years in India as a tea-planter's wife. A keen linguist, Iris learnt Assamese and Gaelic. Among her books are, *The Children of Bird God Hill* (1968), *The Mouth of the Night: Gaelic Stories* (1973), *The Black Hole: Or the Makings of a Legend* (1975) and *Green Gold: The Empire of Tea* (with Alan Macfarlane, 2003). She also wrote for *The Scotsman*, the BBC and *History Today*. She died in 2007.

26954714R00089

Made in the USA
Lexington, KY
22 October 2013